Looking Back
Memories in the Life of a Surgeon

An Autobiography

Eugene R. Celano, M.D.

D1707810

PublishAmerica
Baltimore

First printing

ISBN: 1-4241-7834-7
PUBLISHED BY PUBLISHAMERICA, LLLP
www.publishamerica.com
Baltimore

Printed in the United States of America

Table of Contents

Preface

December 7, 1941 I was still in high school when we heard the news of Pearl Harbor. Some of my older friends, anxious to help, enlisted in the armed services. I was too young, but I couldn't wait until I became of age, when I could enlist. The country was up in arms over the bombing of Pearl Harbor. It was a different world; patriotism was high, and there was very little name calling or opposition to the president. We were at war, a different kind of war, but never the less it was war. All the kids my age wanted to enlist to protect our country.

One of my friends lost his life at Tarawa in the Pacific. It was a shock. Another friend became a Navy pilot, and was assigned to an aircraft carrier flying torpedo bombers. He lost his life in a run toward a Japanese warship while dropping a torpedo. The Japanese destroyed many of our pilots on these runs. They would shoot at the water in front of the incoming torpedo bombers. This created a column of water that the incoming plane would hit, causing the plane to crash. These early experiences created even more of a desire to enlist and do our share.

At age 17, before finishing high school, I enlisted in the Navy flight-training program, but I had to finish school before the Navy would accept me. I couldn't wait. These were exciting times.

The following are memories of experiences I had while in the service of the U.S. Navy and beyond. After spending five years in the service, decisions had to be made. The war was over, and the Navy was trimming down by discharging reserve pilots, of which I was one.

I had to decide on my future, that is, stay in the Navy and take the chance of being discharged before I had enough time in service to earn a retirement, or get out of the Navy and go back to college. I decided to get out, and finish my college education.

The following reflects my experiences for the rest of my life. There are some interesting stories of time spent in medical school, internship and residency, followed by personal experiences in the practice of surgery in a small but growing community.

Chapter One
In the Beginning

I have lived eighty years, and during that time have had many interesting experiences. I've been encouraged to put some of these memories in writing by my wife and some friends. It is difficult to write about oneself, but I think some of these experiences are worth repeating. Having lived to see major changes in the practice of medicine and recalling how medicine was practiced not too many years ago gives me a perspective of how far the world of medicine has come in a short time. I was fortunate to have practiced medicine during a period of time when there were many changes in technology, advances in drug therapy, advances in surgical techniques, and new discoveries. This book is about the career of a young surgeon who came to practice in a small community during this time period.

Everything has a beginning, and it seems appropriate to start with my beginning. I was born in Corona, New York, on February 3, 1926, to two immigrants from Italy. My mother was age two when she arrived at Ellis Island in 1901, and my father came to the new world at age 15 in 1912. He was alone except for an Aunt and Uncle he had never seen before. He served in the United States Army in World War One.

After that, he married my mother, and they lived modestly, to put it mildly, and struggled through the great depression to raise me and my sister. They could only afford two children, and they went through the daily attempts to find work in New York City when jobs were not available. I have memories of my father coming home very depressed, willing to work but unable to find a job. The only alternative for these proud people was to accept welfare. I remember handouts from the welfare department of salt pork, tapioca pudding, and other items from which my mother was able to prepare meals for our family. I recall a Navy peacoat I wore to school given by Welfare—God bless them. Without all of these things I shudder to think of what would have happened to us. My father was restricted because of minimal education and his inability to speak fluent English. He worked hard as a carpenter and cabinet maker, and this was not easy in the cold winters when he had to work outside. He was intelligent enough to realize the importance of an education and always insisted that I continue my schooling.

I worked from the time I was 12 years of age at various jobs. I sold magazines, delivered papers, then all through high school I worked 72 hours a week as a gas station attendant, making $12.00 a week plus tips. Not much, but it helped me buy decent clothes to wear to school. At that time my dad made it clear how he felt about my education. I thought that because I was making so much money that I could quit school. My dad said in his broken English, "I worka with my back—you worka with your head. You quitta the school, and I breaka your head." I got the message from a wise man, and I finished school. It was the best advice I was ever given.

When we were kids, we would buy Bugler tobacco and roll our own cigarettes, or buy Wings cigarettes at ten cents a pack. Then as teenagers we thought it was great fun to go to the woods to smoke. Two of us would smoke up a whole pack of cigarettes before we went home. I am sure that my dad knew when I came home that I had been smoking, so in his usual wisdom, he fixed me up. He said, "Gene, if you want to smoke, don't hide; here is my pipe, my cigarettes, and my chair. Have a ball—go ahead and smoke." That took all of the fun out of it, and I didn't take up smoking again until years later.

Growing up in New York City was, at times, quite difficult. Coming from my Italian background meant that from time to time, I had to stand my ground and assert myself. Kids are cruel and will pick a fight for little or no reason. As the son of an Italian immigrant family, this often created problems, as we were called "Wops," "Dagos," "Guineas," and other names. There was quite an atmosphere of discrimination in those days. This often resulted in a fist fight until the name callers realized that you would stand up for yourself. Then they would leave you alone and go pick on someone else.

This was the situation at my first school, P.S. 30. When I was transferred to P.S. 79, I was a rebellious kid, and I thought I would show them by making lousy grades. I showed them all right. They put me in the "opportunity" class, which was a place to dump all of the dumb kids in that class. That did it! It really pissed me off, and I decided that I would show them. That year was my senior year at that school. I went from being the student with the lowest grades to being the first in my class. At graduation, I was awarded the proficiency medal for being top student, as a reward for my efforts.

I was still rebellious in high school, and for some ridiculous reason that I cannot even remember, about half of the student body went out on strike. That was a bad mistake. We stayed out all day, and went back to class the next day. I think the parents put their foot down, and we were subdued. This participation went on to haunt me later on when I went to enlist in the Navy flight program. The school entered into my high school records that I had participated in a strike against the school, and the Navy enlistment officers considered not letting me into the flight program for that reason. They informed me that I couldn't strike against the Navy. I agreed, and they allowed me to enter the Navy V5 aviation program. I always thought that it was inappropriate for the school to blacken my record for a minor offense. After all, I was just a fourteen-year-old kid that went along with the crowd. I had never had any other disciplinary problems in high school. I thought that it was a dirty trick that could have had serious consequences for the rest of my life. Schools should help guide students as they mature, not seek revenge for childish indiscretions and destroy their futures.

In high school I was an average student not too interested in studies. My interests, and probably one of the reasons I stayed in school, was my participation on the high school swim team where I engaged in numerous activities. I swam one half to one mile a day and in competition. I swam the 50-yard freestyle and 220-yard events. I also filled in for the fancy diving events. Mr. Anthony was a great coach, and the team had great respect for him. We made it to the finals in New York City where our little Bayside High School competed against the best in the city. Our team was great. Our event was a 200-yard-freestyle race. There were four members on a team including me, with each member swimming 50 yards. It's not like it was a photo finish; it wasn't even close. We beat the best in the city by half a pool length, but then came one of my early disappointments—we were disqualified because one official said that I jumped the gun. A rival school official that our school had problems with earlier called it on me. I found out early in life what vindictiveness is all about. To this day, the memory is vivid, and there is no question in my mind that I did not jump too soon. I was the final swimmer in our group and have the satisfaction of knowing that we were the best in the city on that day.

The year was 1943, and we were at war. I was 17 years old and intensely patriotic. Upon graduation I immediately enrolled in the US Navy. I wanted to be a Navy pilot and went into the Navy V5 program to train pilots. I was very disappointed when they did not send me immediately to flight school.

In the meantime I worked for American Airlines for about five months refueling airplanes for the company (DC 3s) and B 24 Liberators for the Air Force. As I recall, they held 4000 gallons of fuel. It took a while to fill those tanks. One of my first airplane rides was given to me by a kind American Airlines pilot on a training flight. He flew over New York City at night. It was quite thrilling.

Another job that I had while waiting to go into the service and right after high school was in Long Island City. It was in a warehouse where items bought at R. H. Macy's were brought together and then distributed to the various boroughs in New York City. The city has five boroughs: Manhattan, Bronx, Staten Island, Brooklyn, and Queens. At this distribution center we loaded truck bodies that were then sent out to be distributed to these areas. The various items were collected in an area between the various truck bodies, and the items were placed or thrown into each truck body. There someone loaded the items and stacked them for shipment.

I happened to be in one truck body, minding my own business and loading the items when the guy distributing the items, instead of throwing them on the floor where I could reach them started to throw them at me, and hitting me. At first I ignored his action and let it go. It then became obvious that his actions were deliberate, and he was looking for trouble. Finally I had taken enough, and I came out to him, slugged him, and knocked him down. The boss came between us and put a stop to it. He said, "What's wrong with you?"

I tried to explain, and said, "If he does it again, I'll knock him on his ass again." With that, we continued our work until out shift was over.

This kid was one of four tough guys from Manhattan, and I was just a young punk from Queens. Interborough rivalry I guess, and for that reason, they disliked me and thought that they could give me a hard time. They were waiting for me outside as I started to go home, and one of them was flashing a knife. They said that they were going to fix me up. I was actually scared to death, but I told them that if they wanted the same treatment their friend had just gotten to come on and try to take me on. I was the smallest one in the crowd, but I was pretty tough and not afraid to fight. Evidently my bluff worked, and they thought better than to try to take me on, and left. I was greatly relieved. They didn't like Italians, and we had to learn to defend ourselves. This was just some of the discrimination that was present in the city at that period of time. I thought that I had seen my last day, but I lucked out.

Shortly after that, the time came for me to enter the service of the United States Navy, and because the flight schools were filled at the time, the Navy decided to send us to college.

I was sent to Dartmouth College for one year, and it turns out that little detour was one of the best things that ever happened to me. It taught me the value of going to college and had a profound effect on the rest of my life.

Chapter Two
Dartmouth College

While at Dartmouth, I took 54 hours of credits in one year; this included courses in chemistry, engineering, and architectural drawing. Also included were math courses: basic math, early and advanced algebra, geometry, trigonometry, spherical trigonometry, navigation, and differential and integral calculus. I loved that school with the winter carnival, outdoor sports, ice statues, and all that went with it! Traditionally at Dartmouth, the students every winter would build huge ice statues of different subjects, and because the winters were so cold, the statues lasted all winter long without melting. There was a rivalry between dormitories, and since the Navy was there at the time, the theme was revolving around military life. One of the statues had a sailor shining a Marine's shoes, again showing the rivalry. Some of these statues were ten feet tall.

The Navy made sure we kept in shape by getting us out of our barracks at daybreak to exercise. We had calisthenics in 20-below-zero weather, and all that we had to wear was a long-sleeved, Navy-issue sweater. No one had to be told to keep moving. The cold was incentive enough. They worked us hard, but it was worth it. It prepared me for future mountains to climb.

Dartmouth became the ninth oldest college in what would later become the United States on December 12, 1769. The charter was written in the name of King George the Third and issued to the New

Hampshire Governor, John Wentworth, as the first college in the royal province of New Hampshire. Later in the 1770s tension between the crown and the colonies began to mount, and Dartmouth proved to be the last colonial college chartered by the British Monarch. Eleazer Wheelock was the driving force in the development of the college. He was dedicated to missionary work, education of earlier settlers, and especially Indians. The symbol of Dartmouth is still the Dartmouth Indian with his "scalplock" haircut. Until recently, native Americans represented 3% of the undergraduate student body. This is the highest percentage of Native Americans among all the highly selective colleges in the country.

A tradition at Dartmouth was their annual winter carnival, at which time the students would enjoy the outdoor life, such as skiing and hiking. They would also be allowed to invite dates for a special weekend to enjoy some social life. Other than that, there wasn't too much to do other than study.

Winter at Dartmouth was very cold, and we had quite a bit of snow. Before the first snowfall the school put out duckboards (wooden platforms to walk on) on the paths across the campus. We wondered why, but we soon found out. When the snow fell it was easy to clear the paths of snow, and when the snow melted in the spring, the paths would fill with water, and we could walk on these boards and keep our feet dry.

My roommates at Dartmouth and I lived together for one year, and most of the time we studied hard, but there were times that we didn't walk the straight and narrow, and we bent the Navy's rules. One such episode was when we were discussing the symbol of Dartmouth, "the Dartmouth Indian," wearing a scalplock haircut. I thought that it was no big deal, so I opened my big mouth and said that I would do that. Naturally, while at Dartmouth I had to show my school spirit, so on a five-dollar bet I got an Indian haircut with a scalplock down the middle. One of my four roommates had been a barber, so he cut my hair. When he got through I had a two inch band of hair from my forehead extending to the back of my neck. The sides were shaven clean and felt as slick as my face after I had finished shaving. It was a piece of art, or so I thought at the time, until I went into the dining room. Remember, I was in the Navy at the time with two thousand sailors, and it made quite a stir.

This did not go over well with the Navy chief in charge of our dormitory. I took a lot of teasing and was made to shave it off; then I looked like Yul Brunner. I had a bald head until it grew back. One year later some of the guys still remembered me as the guy who had the Dartmouth cut.

I went into one of my classes early the next morning, and our professor came in. (It looked like he was hung over.) He took a double take when he saw me. He said, "What the hell is that?" I told him that I was the spirit of Dartmouth. "Oh," he said. The things you do when you are young and foolish.

Seriously, though, Dartmouth is a great school. While there, in one year we had three eighteen-hour-semesters, each lasting four months. Our courses were directed toward math and science and engineering. This was in addition to our daily exercise programs to keep us healthy. Heat power was as difficult a course as I have ever taken. I thought I was going to flunk out after we took the first exam. My score was 5 out of 100, and I thought that was the end of my schooling until I found out that it was the highest grade in the class. Things got better after that.

We had very little time off, so when we had some we raised hell as much as we could on our pay of $28.00 per month that we were given as apprentice seamen. I remember nights (after we ran out of money) hitchhiking back to our barracks with only a sweater, bellbottom trousers, and a Navy peacoat in 20-below weather.

When we did get a chance to get away, usually most of us would head for home. Being stationed at Dartmouth College, I could catch a train from White River Junction, Vermont, to New York City, and then ride the subway and a bus home.

One weekend I came home, and after all of the usual greetings, and renewal of acquaintances, I decided to go out with some of my local friends. We went to one of the local hangouts, and when we were through partying, I headed for home. I had borrowed the family car, which was none too fancy, but my father was kind enough to let me use it. This was during the war, and gas rationing and tire rationing were in effect. It was very difficult to get replacement tires. On the way home I encountered dense fog, and the driving was difficult. Someone before me evidently didn't see the caution light on a street divider island, and had driven over it and knocked it down. When I arrived at the scene, the light was down and out, and I did not see the curb on that island. I hit the curb and blew two tires. I had no spare tires, so I had to pull the car over and park it. I managed to get home about 5:30 the next morning, and had to face the music and tell my dad what had happened. I really hated to break this news because I didn't know where I could replace the tires and didn't know how my dad could get to work the next day.

He took it very well and told me not to worry, that he would find some spare tires. I felt awful and wished that instead of being so understanding, he had just given me hell. I deserved it. Instead he was very supportive. He did find some used tires, we put them on the car, and he was able to use the vehicle again. Another crisis taken care of.

Chapter Three
Early Navy Training

I left Dartmouth on November 1, 1944, to go to the west coast to attend St. Mary's Pre-flight School outside of Oakland, California. There we had six months of intensive training in survival. Most were sports events to build stamina and ego. Competition between battalions in various sporting events was intense. My forte was in swimming, having been on the swimming team at Bayside high school. Most of my competition was from cadets from states where they never saw swimming areas or learned to swim. I swam in every event and won all of them. It was easy, swimming against beginners, but exhausting.

Pre-flight school prepares a naval aviation cadet both physically and mentally for flying airplanes. Courses are given in principles of flight, navigation, engines, airplane recognition, and much more. There is always an emphasis on fitness and survival. Several battalions compete for recognition. Lt. Foreman, our battalion officer, was a great leader, giving us the motivation to excel. Our competition included swimming, track, wrestling, and boxing.

An experience I will never forget was one week on a survival hike. We had to go out into the California wilderness and survive the best we could. We slept in tents and sleeping bags, had hikes, and gathered food and water to supplement our meager diet. Poison oak in California is a formidable enemy to be reckoned with. The Navy decided to experiment with our bodies to keep us from getting poison oak. On this particular excursion, they gave us a derivative of mustard gas to rub on our bodies. Once on, there was no way to get it off except by shower—and there were none available in the wilderness. We lived with this stuff on for a week in so much pain that some cadets actually whimpered in their sleep. (It was really tough on the genitalia!) We did not get poison oak, but I think I would rather have gotten that than to have to be subjected to that pain for a week.

We were on base for three months before they turned us loose to raise hell in San Francisco. We had a well-earned liberty, and after seeing the sights returned to base to finish our pre-flight training. One thrill we had while there was the sight of a Navy SB2C (a bomber) that buzzed the school. It helped us to look forward to completion of our training when we too would be able to fly Navy planes.

After pre-flight school, my next stops were to primary flight school, in Ottumwa, Iowa, and Norman, Oklahoma. There I flew the Navy Stearman (yellow peril). It is a biplane with a 225 hp engine. It is great acrobatic airplane and fun to fly.

In flight training the unexpected can and often does happen. One of these episodes happened to me while flying with a flight instructor in a stearman during primary flight training. The instructor sits in the front seat on this open cockpit airplane, and the student uses the rear seat. Visibility is very limited in that seat because you have to look around the instructor. This instructor had a favorite exercise that he liked to pull on the students. He wanted to see how the student would handle an emergency in the event of an engine failure. He would unexpectedly pull the power off in various situations, and call out ,"Emergency!" over the gosport (communication tube) and the student would then lower the nose of the airplane to prevent stalling, and look for a place to land. After going through this exercise a number of times, he called, "Emergency!" while we were climbing out of a field, and I put the nose down and immediately heard a crashing sound as we hit a tree. We both hit the throttle at the same time, and surprisingly, we were still flying. The only problem was that we had broken off a tree limb about four inches in diameter that was stuck on the landing gear. It formed a "V" with each branch trailing about ten feet behind the airplane. It was really stuck, and in spite of all the instructor's efforts to shake off the branch, he could not shake it off. He had a decision to make. We were glad to be alive, but we couldn't go back to our base with a tree hanging from the landing gear. His decision was to land at an outlying field, let me get out and pull the tree away from where it was stuck on the landing gear, and then go home. It was pretty hairy since he couldn't turn off the engine because we had no way to restart it. So I had to work around removing a very large branch and avoid a whirling propeller. This accomplished, we went back to the base. No more emergencies, and I passed my flight check. No one at the base ever knew what had happened.

After primary flight training, in 1941 I was transferred to Corpus Christi, Texas, for advanced training in the Navy SNJ. This airplane also known as the AT6 in the Air Force. It was a good advanced trainer. It prepared us to fly Navy fighters such as the F6F Hellcat, Corsair, and the F8F Bearcat. It had 600 hp and was a heavier, very stable airplane with a cruise speed of 170 mph. We flew gunnery, bombing, and navigation, missions. We also had plenty of formation flying.

Shortly after arriving at the Naval Air Station Corpus Christi, we had a day or two to look around and familiarize ourselves with the surroundings. We decided to walk through the fields, and found a river that we followed. At some point I decided that I had enough of that fun and decided to make my way back to the highway that was only about 200 yards away. After going about 50 yards toward the road, I was stopped dead in my tracks. A rattlesnake let me know that I had gotten too close. Talk about a sound that will get your attention, and turn your blood cold! The sound of those rattles will do it. I never saw the snake, but I wasn't about to test him. I jumped and quickly returned to the group that was walking along the river bank shouting, "Hey fellows, wait for me!" I was somewhat shaken since I had seen some six-foot rattlesnakes along the road, and they were awesome. They grow them big there. Welcome to Texas.

After completion of our schedule in Corpus Christi, our group was transferred to Pensacola for more advanced training and carrier qualification. At that time two or three of the cadets, including me, owned motorcycles (against Navy regulations). On our days off we would go driving around south Texas at high speeds in the wide-open spaces. When it was time to be transferred, the Navy made arrangements for the cadets to be transferred by train. Our problem was, how do we get our motorcycles to Pensacola nearly 1000 miles away. Two of us decided to skip the train ride drive our motorcycles, and beat the train to the station in Pensacola. What a nightmare that turned out to be! The guy with me had not ever driven a motorcycle, and he was taking this one to Pensacola as a favor to the owner of the cycle. We had to teach him how to drive a motorcycle before we got to Houston. I blew a tire and had to search for a replacement before we left Texas.

That done, we continued on our journey. When we got to Morgan City, Louisiana, we stopped for gas, and my companion made a mistake and put gas in the oil tank. (The two openings were close together.) Because of that I had to have the oil tank drained, replace the oil, and put gas in the proper tank. Then I had to road test the cycle. As I did this, a car pulled in front of me, and I had to lay the motorcycle on its side and slide on the crash bars into and barely under the car. I was not hurt, so we continued on our trip. I was wondering what else this guy was going to do. He was a problem all the way. His cycle was sputtering when we got to New Orleans, and we decided to leave his bike there and let him go to the train station and catch the train. We were still ahead of it. We parked the cycle in the French Quarter and planned to come back later and drive it to Pensacola. From there, I drove on alone almost by instinct. After 800 miles with no stops except for repairs, I was like a zombie and vaguely remember passing cars at night. When I got to Ocean Springs, Mississippi, the engine quit right in front of a funeral home. The people there were glad to keep it for me, so I went to the train station and promptly went to sleep on a bench. While asleep, the train went by, and when I awoke I had no idea how I would get to Pensacola and not be AWOL. Fortunately I was able to catch a bus and get there before the train. I was waiting at the station when the train arrived, and I looked like hell. I had been through it. God was with me, or I would never have gotten that far.

I still do not know how I made it. Two weeks later I went back to get the bike and all that was wrong was a break on an insulator in the distributor. I fixed the problem and then drove back to Pensacola. Riding a motorcycle that far is no picnic. It is very exhausting.

Chapter Four
Pensacola and Advanced Flight Training

After that, I was transferred to Pensacola, Florida, for further training and to eventually receive my Navy Wings of Gold. That was a proud day when that happened. Further training in Pensacola was continued in the SNJ and included night flying, formation flying, gunnery, and other activities. This was carried out at Bloody Barin Field (so called because of the number of cadets that were lost there in flight training). Carrier qualification practice on land was carried out at Saufley Field before landing aboard the *USS Saipan,* a cruiser converted to an aircraft carrier. Was that ever small! We had to make twenty-five takeoffs and landings to qualify. I qualified in the SNJ and later the F6F Hellcat on that tiny excuse for an aircraft carrier.

My next tour of duty was when I transferred to Banana River NAS (now Cape Canaveral) in Florida. It is now known as Patrick Air Force Base. There we became familiar with the Grumman F6F Hellcat, a single-seated fighter. This airplane was carrier based and was very active during the war. It was powered by a Pratt and Whitney 2000 hp engine that gave it a top speed of 380 mph. This was quite respectable in those days. It had six wing-mounted 50-caliber machine guns that held 2400 rounds of armament. It also had excellent range, carrying 250 gallons of fuel in self-sealing tanks and 150 gallons in a drop tank. During the war, the F6F proved itself; its awesome firepower and pilots were responsible for destroying 5000 enemy aircraft with a loss ratio of 19 to 1 in our favor.

We became very familiar with the aircraft before we were allowed to fly it, and since it was a single-seater, we had to learn about the F6F only in flight manuals. Then when you climbed into the cockpit you were blindfolded and required to know where all of the instruments and various levers such as flaps and landing gear were. Then you were on your own. After that, we climbed into the airplane and tested our skills by flying alone. Our group, called the Barflies, had seven pilots and an instructor assigned to us. Whitey Holmguard was our mentor, and he took us through our paces, including instrument flying, gunnery practice, formation flying, and carrier qualification on the *USS Saipan*, in Pensacola. If you could land on this, you could land on anything. We also trained over the Atlantic Ocean and the Everglades.

In those days there were no "G" suits (used to increase pressure on the legs and abdomen to help prevent blackouts). Blackouts occur when an aircraft pulls Gs, such as after a steep dive and then a rapid pullout. One G equals your body weight, and four Gs equals four times your body weight. Pilots had to be in good condition when flying to withstand four-to-five Gs before blacking out. This happened frequently on gunnery runs when a pilot would make a steep run on a target, pull 5-to-6 Gs on the pullout, and black out. It was like pulling a window shade in front of your eyes; you were aware of your flight attitude, but you could see nothing but black. At that point, you just maintained your heading, hoping no one was in your way, and in fifteen or twenty seconds, depending on the severity of the pullout, your vision returned. It was quite an experience the first time, but you soon adjusted to it and knew what to expect the next time.

We also trained in night flying, and that's where I encountered my first case of vertigo. While flying wing on our instructor over the Everglades and watching the flame from his exhaust, it was hypnotic, and I lost my sense of up and down. It felt as if we were flying upside down. He was far more experienced than I was, so believing in him, fortunately I kept my formation rather than believe my feelings and breaking off. It was pitch dark, and when we turned back toward ground lighting, I reestablished my sense of up and down. Had I not done that I would have been a statistic.

As members of the squadron, we were each assigned different duties that were necessary to keep the squadron functioning. My job was test pilot. After an airplane came out of maintenance, (engine change, etc.) it was my job to test the airplane and fly it through all of its capabilities. It was an exciting job, and I was to report any discrepancies before the airplane was put back into service. I tested the gear, flaps, all of the engine instruments, manifold pressure, rpm, full speed, high altitude capability, and the oxygen system. I took an F6F to 45,000 feet to where it would not climb another inch. It's not supposed to fly that high, but there it was. It was a great airplane.

My next tour of duty was in Quonset Point, Rhode Island, where it was my good fortune to be assigned to squadron VF8A. My squadron was assigned to the Essex Class Carrier *USS Leyte* for about two years, where I flew F8F Bearcats, (hottest thing going at the time. The first model to come off the assembly line was the F8F1, and it was a superb airplane. It carried four 50-caliber machine guns, had a top speed of 421 mph, and a range of two thousand miles. It could climb to ten thousand feet in ninety seconds. We flew these airplanes for several months with no problems, and then the Navy decided to improve them. The new F8F2 was improved by lengthening the rudder; that added stability. Four 20-mm cannons were added instead of the 50-caliber machine guns, for additional fire power. We were the first squadron to receive the new product, and we were eager to try out our new toy. It flew pretty much the same as the F8F1, but we had some problems. As long as the power was on, it was fine, but when the power was cut, as in approaching the airport to land, the engine would quit. This would force us to come in to the field high and fast so that we could glide and still make the runway. It was not unusual to see three or four airplanes sitting on the runways with dead engines until they could be restarted and taxied back to our assigned area. We flew these airplanes under those conditions for a few months until they were all recalled to fix the problem. It was a bit unnerving because the glide ratio on the airplane was not too good when landing deadstick. I used to say that the glide ratio was 11 to 1 in reverse. You had to be 11 miles high to glide one mile. (That was a joke, but it wasn't too far off.)

Another problem we had at Quonset Point was fighting the problems with the cold weather. The runways would sometimes become icy, and when landing, it could be quite an experience. Trying to taxi on ice was a challenge. We had one mechanic who was running an engine for testing, and because of the ice on the tarmac, and the running of the powerful engine, he jumped the chocks, and chewed up the back half of an airplane that was parked in front of him. Needless to say, that was one lost airplane.

One cold day at Quonset Point we were preparing for a flight. It is necessary and required to check the airplane for fuel and flyability. Most of us flew the flight with no problem, but a friend, Red Kennedy, was not so fortunate. It was customary in checking for fuel to flip on the fuel gauge to check the fuel level in the tank. He did this, and it read "full" before his flight. What happened was that the airplane, which is supposed to be refueled after each flight, had not been refueled. The gauge that erroneously read full was frozen from the cold, and he took off with minimal fuel. As a result he ran out of gas and crashed. He survived, but suffered a broken back and was then through with his flying career. Moral of the story is: disregard the fuel gauge, and always check the tanks.

While at Quonset Point, Rhode Island, and flying the F8F Bearcat, we performed in several different activities designed to keep up our proficiency. We fired on tow targets with marked bullets, so that we could later see who scored and hit the target and who did not, when the target sleeve was brought back to base and analyzed. We used various bombing targets on which we dropped small bombs that on impact would put off a smoke puff so that you could see how close you were to the target. We even used this exercise on submarines coming out of New London, Connecticut. They cooperated with us in the training exercises.

Another exercise or play time was flying "tail chase." At that time, we would have six-to-eight airplanes in a flight, and we played follow the leader. If the leader did a slow roll, all the airplanes followed and did a slow roll; if the leader did a loop, we all followed his lead. This was a dangerous maneuver, because if all the airplanes in the flight didn't keep up their speed in the loop, the plane behind could catch up to the plane he was following, resulting in a mid-air collision. We flew close together, and if the maneuver wasn't flown completely smoothly by all the pilots, and one pulled back too vigorously on the stick, it slowed down his airplane, and the plane behind him could catch up and chew up his tail. This very thing happened to me one day while we were tail chasing and completing a loop. I was the last plane in the flight, and as I pulled up to the top of the loop, the plane ahead of me had slowed down, and with the speed of my plane, I came very close to overrunning him. All I could see as I came around was a windshield full of his airplane. We were very close, and instinctively I pulled the stick back into my lap and came out of the loop. How I missed him I will never know, but at the time, I guess the good Lord was looking after me. It is as close as I ever came to a mid-air collision. It could have been my last day in this world.

Chapter Five
Experience on the *USS Leyte*

In the two years while assigned to the Aircraft Carrier *USS Leyte*, we went to Argentia, New Foundland, the Mediterranean, and the Caribbean. While at sea, we flew every day on different missions. Looking back, some of the things we did were dangerous and downright foolish, but we obeyed orders and did as we were told.

One such experience on the carrier was to lift a tow target off the ship for the flights to practice gunnery. The tow target had a line that was 500 feet long, placed on the flight deck and attached to the airplane preparing for takeoff. The tow target was white and about six feet wide. Each plane had different colored bullets in their ammo, so that at the end of the flight when the banner was brought on deck, the bullet holes were counted, and each pilot received a score. It was very competitive.

To take the banner into the air, we would take turns so that each pilot had his scare or turn. The plane was put on the catapult with the line attached. The brakes were held, head back on the headrest, full power applied, and the catapult was shot (released). As you approached the end of the catapult (barely flying speed) you would retract the gear and go straight up to 500 ft., and then level off. The target was then pulled off the flight deck, and away you went. I don't know whose idea this was: probably some non-flying admiral. I don't know of another airplane that could do this without stalling, and if you stalled, with the ship going under you, the airplane would come crashing back on the flight deck. This was a thrilling but very dangerous maneuver. Only because the F8F had so much power were we able to get away with it. We were young and didn't know that it was dangerous. We thought it was great fun.

One day while our group was shooting at the target, we were called to return to the ship. I was the last plane in the flight, and I wanted to make my last run a good one, so I fired my guns right on down to the target. The carrier was turning into the wind, and the wind was at my back as I fired. When I landed and we went back to the ready room for debriefing, the air group commander was there, and he asked who the last plane in the flight was, and I proudly put my hand in the air, thinking that I was going to be complemented for my last run. He tossed a 20-mm, one-pound shell casing to me and said, "You dropped six of these on the flight deck on your last run." I am lucky that no one on the flight deck was hurt. The combination of the ship turning back into the wind, and the wind behind me brought the shells over the deck. I knew that I was in big trouble, but all he said was "Nice run. Dismissed." I put my tail between my legs and left, not knowing whether to be proud or embarrassed.

Navy pilots are trained and proud of their skills of precision flying. This is very important when making carrier landings. In those days, the Navy had not, as yet, advanced to the larger slant-deck carriers with plenty of landing area. Although our carrier was 800 feet long, we could only make safe landings on about 300 feet of carrier deck before hitting a barrier. The barrier is made up of steel cables that will stop an airplane if it lands too long. This is designed to protect the airplanes that are stacked forward of the barriers. We qualified for carrier landings on a converted cruiser on which the deck is much shorter than on our ship. It was even more of a challenge.

Normally when there is a routine approach to landing, the pilot approaches the ship parallel to it but going in the opposite direction. He puts down his gear and flaps, checks his altitude of 100 feet, makes sure his fuel selector is on the main tank, drops his tailhook, opens and locks his canopy, puts the prop in full low pitch, (in case of a waveoff) and prepares to land. He starts his 180-degree turn when he is opposite the stern of the ship, and turns until he picks up the paddles of the landing signal officer (LSO), about halfway through the turn. From then on, the pilot's life is in his hands, and the pilot follows his directions without question. He tells the pilot through his paddles if he is on a proper flight path, if he is high or low, fast or slow, and at the right moment he gives the pilot a "cut." The pilot then takes off all power and lands. If he waves the pilot off, he adds full power and goes around again for another try. Fortunately, this didn't happen too often, and although our ship was 800 feet long, we were only able to use the first three cables on landing without hitting a barrier. The barrier protected airplanes parked forward of it. Today's modern carriers have the benefit of a slant deck and 1000 feet of landing area, and their procedure is to hit full throttle upon landing, so that if they fail to catch a wire they can easily go around for another try. We didn't have that option.

These landing signal officers were our friends and were highly respected. If he gave us a waveoff, we never questioned his authority; we went around again. There could have been a barrier crash or foul deck, and we didn't want to land on someone. After landing, the tailhook is removed, the barriers are dropped, the pilot taxies forward rapidly, and the barrier is put back up in preparation for the next airplane's landing. All of this takes place in less than 30 seconds. There is no time to waste; the ship is trying to take about 100 airplanes aboard. The pilot must catch one of the first three cables; if he catches cable number four he is in the barrier. If he hits a barrier with the F8F, unless his tailhook caught a landing cable, the airplane flipped over on its back, which was not too healthy for plane or pilot. There is an old saying in the Navy among carrier pilots: "There are only two types of carrier pilots, those who have had a barrier crash, and those who were going to get one." I was fortunate enough to accumulate 100 carrier landings without an accident.

I flew as wingman on a fellow pilot named Sarris. He was experienced and very well qualified. This is important when landing an aircraft on a carrier, especially when you have 100 aircraft, are low on fuel, and ready to land one at a time. It was almost routine with him.

I knew and trusted him and knew just how long it would take him to make his approach and land. I knew that when he turned in toward the carrier that he would land, have his tailhook retracted, taxi forward past the barriers, have the barriers elevated for the next landing, and I would be clear to land. Thirty seconds after he landed I would be landing, having my tail hook released, and moving forward of the barriers so that the next plane was free to land. It worked like a charm, but it meant that we had to have a lot of confidence and trust in each other. Sometimes too much.

On this flight where I was wingman, I was flying along, fat, dumb, and happy, and trusting my leader, when he signaled to me that his radio had gone out. Great! Here we were, three hours into the flight in the middle of the Mediterranean, out of sight of land, and he turned over the lead (and the fate of our group of airplanes) to me. I didn't have a clue where we were! Fortunately we had a signal device installed in the plane that if used properly would lead us back to the ship. I picked a heading, and crossed my fingers, and after about thirty minutes with sweaty palms, we found the carrier, much to my relief.

During my tour on the *Leyte* I had several exciting experiences and some not so exciting. We lost our skipper and another squadron mate on an approach to the carrier. I happened to be watching them at the time when they lost flying speed on the turn into the landing and flew into the sea. They both came in too low and slow and stalled. Another pilot on his approach was out of position, and took a wave off. When he added power, the torque from the powerful R-2800 Pratt and Whitney engine turned him upside down, and he went into the sea next to the carrier. As we watched, it seemed like an eternity, but in about one to two minutes, he blew up his Mae West and popped to the surface. We were certainly relieved, and he was unhurt. When he came back aboard ship, he turned in his wings and went back to the non-flying regular Navy. He said he had enough of carrier flying.

John Burnett was another squadron mate who survived a crash close to the carrier. He called the ship and told them he had engine trouble and needed to land. The carrier turned into the wind and prepared to have him land. As he turned toward the ship, his engine quit, and he went into the drink short of the carrier. He was a big man, but he immediately got out of the cockpit and inflated his Mae West. A crowd of us had gathered on the flight deck cheering him on, and when he went in, we all were elated to see him clear the airplane so soon. The plane sank in about 20 seconds, and the escort destroyer brought him back to the ship unharmed and able to fly again. The destroyer crew was rewarded with many gallons of ice cream from the carrier for the rescue. This was a Navy tradition for rescuing one of our pilots.

Landing an airplane without flaps to slow you down is not a big deal on land. I have done that several times, but on a carrier, landing without flaps is a big deal. Flaps not only give you the ability to slow the airplane down, but they create more lift, enable you to fly slower, and give you an extra cushion to guard against stalling the airplane as you make the approach. Stalling at that low altitude usually turns the airplane over on its back, and there is no hope for recovery.

I had occasion to land on the carrier with no flaps, which means your stalling speed is higher on approach—a frightening situation. The carrier had just finished launching about 80 airplanes, and once they do that, they are not too anxious to land any airplanes until the flight is over, four hours later. Fifteen minutes into the flight I began to lose all of my hydraulic fluid. It was sloshing around in the cockpit, and fortunately, I had presence of mind to put on my goggles to protect my eyes. Hydraulic fluid in the eyes is not exactly healthy, and you must see to land the airplane. I called the ship and told them I had an emergency and had to land. I was able to drop the gear, which I did immediately, but I was not able to extend my flaps. The F8F had to be brought into the carrier normally at higher speeds, because when power was cut to land, the weight of the heavy engine would cause the nose would drop, resulting in blown tires and buckled wings. We would bring it in at more speed so that we could fly the airplane to the deck, keeping the nose high. We would fly it in normally at 110 miles per hour. On this approach, because I had no flaps, I had to bring it in at 125-130 miles per hour to prevent stalling. I flew a good approach, because I knew that I would not get a second chance. I cut the power and prayed I wouldn't bounce and miss catching a wire. When I caught #2 cable, the sudden stoppage splashed hydraulic fluid all over the cockpit and me. I was soaked, but I had saved the airplane and more important to me, the pilot. It had to be a perfect approach and landing that day.

Just when I was congratulating myself for a successful landing, I got a call to the bridge to talk to the executive officer. There he proceeded to chew me out for ending the flight early. He wanted to know why I came in so soon. I didn't say a word. He was facing the flight deck while talking to me and. When I didn't answer him, he turned around to face me. There was a slight pause, he looked at me, soaking wet in my flight suit, and said, "Oh! Dismissed."

Sometimes later, I was on the bridge watching landings when this same executive officer came in to land, and he was too fast; he missed all of the wires, hit a barrier, and turned upside down right in front of me. Fortunately he hit the deck on the overturn structure on the airplane, and all he ended up with was a slight concussion..

While on the carrier *Leyte*, we cruised and flew all over the Mediterranean. We went to Gibralter, Nice, and Cannes on the coast of France, to Naples, Malta, Crete, Greece, Turkey, and Algiers.

While in Naples I had the opportunity to visit my grandfather, who was 85 years old, living in Agrigento, Sicily. My father had died the year prior to my visit, and I had never seen my grandfather. After my father immigrated to the US at age 15 he never again saw his father, so this visit was something special. I took a ship overnight to Palermo, Sicily, from Naples; then from there I hired a car and two people to escort me ninety miles to Agrigento. When I got there, my grandfather could not believe it; he was overjoyed. I looked very much like my father, and it was an emotional meeting. I was in my naval uniform, and he proudly showed me around the small town. He was amazed that I made the trip alone because Sicily was such a dangerous place. My command of the Italian language was not too good, but we managed to have a very nice visit. I left the next day, and he insisted on going back to Palermo with me to protect me. It was a trip that I will long remember.

Another interesting memory was when I had chance to have an audience with Pope Pius XII. Eight of the ship's officers, including me, were invited to meet with him at Castle Gondolfo in Rome in a private meeting with just the eight of us. He visited with us for 30 minutes or so, gave us each a religious medal and wished us well. It was quite a memorable experience.

While on the French Riviera we also had a chance to visit the Casino at Monte Carlo. It's not like casinos in the United States, in that it is very quiet. We even got to play some blackjack. There is some very serious gambling that goes on there.

We also saw some interesting sights on the beach at Cannes. One day I was reporting on deck for my watch, but the guy I was to relieve did not want to be relieved. I saw him looking at the shore through a set of huge binoculars (part of the ship's equipment fastened to the deck). When I got a chance to look, I saw why he did not want to be relieved. He was watching all the nude bathers on the beach: quite a sight. The French thought nothing of it, but for us sailors who had been at sea for four months, it got our attention.

The last tour I had on the *Leyte* was to the Carribean. I was flying as wingman with my skipper on one of my last flights before leaving the ship. He ran the belly tank dry, and the engine quit. This is common. When it happens you switch to your main tank, and the engine will usually restart. This time it didn't restart. I followed him down from altitude while he worked frantically to restart the engine, and it finally restarted just before he went into the water. He was getting ready to ditch, and we were both really relieved, and headed back to the ship.

I have lived in Florida most of my life and have been through many hurricanes. They can be frightening, but none has been nearly as bad as a hurricane the *USS Leyte* went through in the north Atlantic. The storm had 75-to-80-mile-an-hour winds, causing waves that were 50 feet high. All that the carrier could do was maintain headway by keeping the ship pointed into the wind. We were in the storm for 10 days and were blown 750 miles off course. The ship would ride over one wave, then shake and drop the bow into the next on-coming wave. Green water, not just spray, would come over the bow and pour into the hangar deck which was about 150 feet from the bow. On the stern, standing there and rocking, one minute you were 70 feet above the water, and the next minute it came so close you could reach out and touch the sea. The ship has expansion joints in the middle, and they were sliding back and forth as much as a foot as the ship rocked. We lost several "I" beams as wide as two feet across. The ship took such a beating that it had to go into dry dock when we returned to our home port of Quonset Point.

After my tour of duty in the Navy of five years, I was transferred to Pensacola for my discharge. When I received my orders on the ship, I still wanted to fly my last flight in an F8F, but the skipper would have none of it. He said he didn't want anything to happen to me on my last flight. Life is full of disappointments, so I had to comply. When my orders for transfer were written, no priority was given for a flight to Pensacola. Without a priority I could have been stuck in Guantanamo Bay Naval Air Station for weeks until someone gave me a ride home, and this would have put me in a difficult situation. This was early September, and school started in mid-September. If I were delayed, I would have to put off starting school for about five months. The flights leaving Guantanamo Bay for the states were not full, but the small technicality of no priority would prevent me from getting off the island. I solved that problem by retyping my orders and inserting the word "priority." I was then able to leave the next day! I don't know what would have happened if I had been found out, but I felt it was worth the risk. The flight from Cuba landed in Jacksonville, Florida, but I still needed to get to Pensacola. Fortunately I met a Navy pilot that needed a copilot to fly a DC3 to Pensacola; I immediately volunteered.

Chapter Six
Pre-Med and Medical School

My discharge came a few weeks later, but I was allowed to start school before I was released. I was one of about 35 students attending the first-year of the new Pensacola Junior College in 1948. I had credit for 54 hours at Dartmouth College so I was able to graduate in one year in June of 1949 with an AA degree. I was the first class president and chancellor of the first honor court. (Big deal—there were only four in the first class). The school is now 58 years old and has greatly expanded into a first-rate junior college.

From there I was off to Tulane University in New Orleans for their summer school program in pre- med training and admission to Tulane University School of Medicine. Because Pensacola Junior College was a new college, in order to meet the requirements for pre-med, I had to repeat some of the courses. Another disappointment. I continued at Tulane until early 1951 when I was accepted into Tulane Medical School.

At that time, having met all of the requirements for pre-med, and having a family to support, I spent about six months selling insurance. I did well, but it wasn't fun chasing down people to pay their weekly premiums. It was a living, and I needed to survive.

Starting medical school was a real thrill to me. I felt that they had gotten to the bottom of the barrel when they picked me, but I worked hard and was persistent, and I finished. Tulane is a great school, and I did well in spite of the fact that I was married and had two children.

36

Going to school married, trying to raise kids on 28 dollars a month of G.I. Bill and a small amount of help from the family was no picnic. Under the best of circumstances pre-med and later medical school takes a lot of work and determination. Not only do you have to provide your own food and lodging, but you have to keep up with your grades so that when you apply to medical school for admission, you have a chance of being accepted. Tulane is a well-known, highly respected school, and every year there are several thousand very good applicants from all over the country.

The competition is very keen. You also have to spend some time with your family as well as take time to study. I nearly lost my opportunity while in pre-med. I was taking genetics which was a required course for acceptance to medical school. I had been a good student, with a high B average, but when I saw the final exam, I just went blank. I had recently been through some very serious marital problems and was not able to think. I could not even answer one question. After about twenty minutes, I handed the professor a blank paper and he said, "What's this?" at which time I broke down and told him about my problems. Fortunately this wonderful man had been through similar problems and was very sympathetic. God bless him! He handed the test paper back to me and said to go back and do the best that I could. With his encouragement I was able to go back and finish the exam and get a B+ in the course. Without his help and compassion there is no way that I could have overcome failing a required course and still be accepted into medical school. When I applied for entrance into medical school it would have been all over. I have since then had the greatest admiration for professors and teachers, knowing how much of an influence they can have on a student's future.

While at Tulane, during my pre-med studies, I found time to participate in naval reserve duties, and as an ex-naval aviator, I was qualified to fly with the reserve unit at Lakefront New Orleans Airport. We were nicknamed "weekend warriors" and flew Navy Corsairs, (also known as the Bent Wing Widow Maker). We flew training missions over Lake Pontchatrain, missions designed to keep up our proficiency in navigation, formation flying, gunnery, and bombing. The type of airplane we flew had been used extensively during the war in the Pacific, especially by the Marines. Pappy Boyington of the Marines shot down 26 Japanese airplanes in a Corsair. It was fast, and it was deadly, in more ways than one. Several early trainees, including a personal friend of mine, died in this type of airplane. At slow speeds, it was notorious for turning upside down on an approach when the pilot had no time to recover. Moral of the story is: don't fly the Corsair too close to stall speed on an approach to the runway or a carrier.

While flying this airplane, I had a few exciting moments, or shall I say there was never a dull moment! On a trip our group made from New Orleans to Miami, three of us landed at Tyndall Air Force Base in Panama City, Florida, to refuel and then go on to Miami. On the way to Miami, while over the everglades, my cylinder head temperature gauge went out of sight into redline figures. I could just see me bailing out over the everglades, being eaten by alligators and never found. I decided that I would fly the bird as far as it would go before bailing out. I just knew that with the high temperature on this single-engine airplane that the engine would freeze before I reached Miami, but I made it to Opelica Airport and landed safely. Examination by maintenance revealed a defective cylinder head temperature gauge and no problems with the engine. I was one relieved pilot and later flew the same airplane back to our home base in New Orleans.

Another interesting episode happened on a night flight in New Orleans. It was an exceptionally cold night, and there was no heat in the airplane. When we finished our flight and returned to base, there was a brush fire at the airport, and we were not allowed to land until the ground crew had put the fire out. After circling for an hour, I was numb, and had to land on a crosswind runway. The Corsair does not do well on crosswind landings because the wind has a tendency to get under the wing, lift it up, and that combined with the long nose turn the airplane into the wind. This particular runway is next to the water, and when I landed, the Corsair tried to turn toward the water. I held it by holding the left brake until it came under control, and then I taxied in.

The next morning I checked the tire, and as a result of holding the brake the night before, I had worn through 7 of the 8 plies of the tire. One more ply and I would have been swimming on a frigid night. I had just been accepted for entrance to Tulane Medical School, and the Navy told me to stay in the reserves and most likely go to Korea, or resign and go to school. After all the years and effort to get into medical school, I regretfully resigned. It was a tough choice, but I had a family to support. Aviation was a big part of my life, but I had to give it up at that time for a few years.

In my first year in medical school, the courses included gross anatomy, microanatomy, neuroanatomy, biochemisty, and physiology.

Going to medical school is not easy. The hours are long, and after school it takes many hours of study to keep up and digest all of the material presented in classes. Most of the students were single and went directly into medical school after college and pre-med. Some of us had spent some time in the service and were married with children. It made it very difficult to study. Usually I would get home at five thirty, eat dinner, spend some time with the kids, and then try to study. By then it was eight thirty or so at night, and it was difficult after a long day to study. I would sit in a chair trying to study and fall fast asleep. The single students had a real advantage, and since they had no family obligations, they could start studying much earlier, before they were totally exhausted. A very good friend of mine, Parky Parkinson, and I studied together. He had no young kids, so I went to his apartment where it was quiet, and we could study. It was good for both of us. We had a quiet place to study, and we helped each other learn. We made coffee so strong to try to stay awake that we kiddingly said we had to cut it with a knife rather then pour it. Also, to try to stay awake, we would stand up and read our notes to each other. This worked pretty well, but often while standing and reading, I would go to sleep and have to be awakened. It was hard work. It was a tough year for me, being married with two children at the time and serious marital problems. I finished the first year in 27th place out of 134 in the class. The good Lord was looking over me! The first two years were spent at the uptown medical school on the Tulane Campus, and the last two years were spent downtown, next to the huge charity hospital of New Orleans. There were approximately 3000 beds there, and we were able to use the facilities of the hospital. We were exposed to an unbelievable volume of patients with almost every disease known to man. It was a great learning institution.

Medical school is very intensive and stressful, but on occasion we did have time for some foolishness. In the first year we were assigned to a large room full of cadavers. These were bodies of people that were unknown and abandoned, and they were used to train students in anatomy. You start out by having to skin the body, then gradually dissect out all of the muscle groups, blood vessels, nerves, and organs. All of this is done while trying to retain your composure over the heavy smell of formaldehyde that the cadaver has been embalmed in. This is where out of a class of 134 we lost half a dozen students. They couldn't quite hack it. Each cadaver had four medical students assigned to it, and they worked together as a team in the dissection process.

Our cadaver happened to be at the entrance to the lab, so that anyone coming in to the lab to work on their cadaver had to come right by our table. There were four girls in our class, and we had good relations with all of them. One of the girls, Mary Flynn, had an exceptionally white complexion, and we decided to have some fun with Mary. Our cadaver was a male, and we decided to put a string on his well-endowed penis, and put the end of the string in the abdomen ready for action. We called it the "Flynn ligament." When Mary came by our table, we pulled on the string and created an erection. Her white complexion turned bright red, and we cracked up. When she had to go in and out of the room, she would stay as far away from us as she could. It was a cruel joke, but she was a good sport and didn't report us, and we finally had to abandon our antics. It was fun while it lasted.

Periodically we had a test in the anatomy lab that consisted of the instructor putting a label on the various structures on the cadaver. It was then up to the students to read the label, write the name on our exam sheet, and identify which structure was labeled. Our instructor, Dr. Reed, was a wonderful man, an ex-wrestler, who occasionally would play a practical joke on a student. The last thing he said before turning the students loose on identification was to tell us in no uncertain terms, that we were not to touch the labels under any circumstances. Well, guess what? The first label I came to was turned upside down, and impossible to read. I did everything but stand on my head to try to read the cotton-pickin' label. Finally in desperation, I reached over to turn the label up to where I could read it, and that did it. Dr. Reed slapped his heavy hand on my back, and I thought I had been shot. I know that he did this on purpose to prove a point, but this student was so rattled after that, that it was hard to think. I passed the exam, but it was close.

Our class had some strange characters in it. One day we were dealing with live frogs in our microbiology lab, and someone came up with the idea of eating frogs. Who would do such a thing! Well, one of the students said he would for a price. Several of us got together and collected twenty-seven dollars to watch him eat a live frog. He proceeded to bite the frog's head off, and then swallow the rest of the frog. Our group gathered around him to watch, and the last thing we saw was the frog's legs kicking as it went into his mouth. We gave him the twenty-seven dollars, but it nearly cost him his medical school career. Money was tight amongst medical students, but this was going a bit too far.

My very good friend and classmate and I, Barnard Russell, decided to pull a prank on a preacher who was a student in our clinical lab class. Bob Hess was a good sport, and at the time we were studying blood serology, specifically syphilis. We each had to stick our finger to get a blood sample, put it under the microscope, and determine whether or not we had syphilis or positive serology. We thought it would be great sport to switch slides with our preacher friend and instead of him looking at his own blood sample, we would have him looking at one that was positive for syphilis. Well! This created quite a reaction. His face reddened, he was flustered, and called the instructor for verification. She was not too happy, and a repeat sample showed he was negative. She then wanted to know who was behind this evil deed. "Raise your hand, or I'll flunk the entire class." Barnard and I decided to fess up and take our punishment and raised our hands. When we looked around, all the students in the class had raised their hands. In frustration, she threw up her hands and said, "Okay, go back to work and never let this happen again." During one of these tests that we were running on ourselves, one of our classmates diagnosed himself. He had leukemia.

The last two years of medical school were spent in downtown New Orleans at the charity hospital and the downtown medical school. As I mentioned before, every illness and condition could be seen at this facility. New Orleans is a port city, and in addition to the usual illnesses seen in the United States we got to see patients with all kinds of tropical diseases. At that time, the charity hospital also had an infectious disease center and a polio center. This was in the days before the discovery of the Salk vaccine, and it was heartbreaking to see these pathetic children. Many of them remained paralyzed for life. Thank God for the discovery of the vaccine.

While at Charity, we had patients assigned to us for evaluation and recommended treatment. The only problem was that the medical student was so low on the totem pole that to get a nurse to help examine a female patient was impossible. Imagine the consequences in our present litigious society. I had a female patient assigned to me who came from the French Quarter. In those days the French Quarter was a wild place inhabited by some very wild women. This young lady was quite pretty but a bit on the wild side. I did my best to be very professional, had her undress, gave her a gown, and had her lie down on the exam table so that I could perform a physical examination. All went well as I examined her ears, eyes, nose, throat, neck, breasts, and abdomen. Still no nurse in sight to help me, but I still had to do a pelvic exam, so I helped put her feet in stirrups and prepared to do a pelvic exam. I needed to check her uterus, tubes, and ovaries, and as I inserted my exam fingers into her vagina, it all started. She began to bump and grind, and twist and turn. What a revolting development this was. It startled me, and here I am with no nurse, needing to do this exam for a grade, and I run into an oversexed woman. I asked her to please stop, that I had to do this for a grade, and at this time about all

I could tell was that it was warmer inside the vagina than it was outside. She settled down, and I finished the exam a little shaken by this unusual and unexpected event.

One of my classmates had an unusual and embarrassing occurrence while examining one of his male patients at Charity Hospital. As I had mentioned earlier, we had no nurses to assist us and had to do all of the exams by ourselves. We wore lab coats to make us look like real doctors, and also to keep us from staining our own clothes. This day while trying to perform a rectal exam on his patient, he had the patient bend over the table so that he could go ahead with the exam. He placed one hand on the patient's back, and then tried to insert his gloved finger into the patient's rectum, but to no avail. He couldn't get his finger into the patient's rectum. He looked down and saw his necktie draped over his gloved finger preventing him from entering the rectum. Embarrassed, he cut off his necktie and proceeded with the examination. It took a long time for him to live this down, and we teased him unmercifully. From then on, he wore no more neckties, only bow ties.

We had duty in the emergency room where we learned about the trauma that goes on nightly in the big city of New Orleans. I had to sew lacerations, but the first time is not too easy. Even though you practice knot tying at home, when it comes to sewing on a live patient it takes some practice. My first victim was an experienced night fighter, who had been sewn up in the emergency room many times before, so when I started my clumsy knot tying, he knew that I was a novice and wanted another doctor. I calmed him down and finished the job, learning from the experience, but slightly embarrassed. There was a great improvement in my knot tying after that.

One night I volunteered to go on an ambulance call, which was in the French Quarter, at the court of two sisters. A young lady had taken an overdose and was comatose. The intern on ambulance duty did his best to revive her, but to no avail. She died after reaching the hospital.

I took some time off for recreation on Wednesday afternoons to try to keep my sanity. At that time the school taught elective courses that were not part of the medical school curriculum, and many students took these elective courses. I told my friends that my elective was golf, and that it met on the first tee at city park at one o'clock each Wednesday, and anyone that wanted to join me for my elective could meet me at the golf course. Each Wednesday I would leave for school (which we had until noon) with my golf clubs under one arm and my books under the other. One day, Barnard saw me going to school with my golf clubs and he said to me "Are you crazy? We have a pathology final tomorrow." I said I had to meet my elective and headed off to the golf course.

Dr. Alton Ochsner was one of our loved and respected professors. Every week he held a teaching session in an amphitheater. We called it the bullpen. There cases were presented to him by a student, who was then questioned by him about the physical findings and details about the patient's disease or condition. This really put the student on the spot, with all of his classmates looking down on him. The cases were varied and unusual. One day he brought in a patient who had "situs inversus." This patient's organs were reversed internally, and he had typical symptoms of gall bladder disease, but on the wrong side. The student did an excellent job of presentation, but was puzzled by the physical findings, and Dr. Ochsner was having some fun with him. The student said it sounds just like gallbladder disease, but the symptoms are on the wrong side. Then Dr. Ochsner revealed to the student what the unusual situation was, and we all had a big laugh.

Dr. Ochsner was tough, but he loved the medical students, and we knew it. There was a story about a case that he was operating on for cancer of the lung, and he wanted his residents to feel the tumor. This was a sterile operating room, and he and his assistants were fully gowned and gloved. The medical student stood behind him as an observer with no gloves on. Dr. Ochsner said, "Look at this tumor; I want you to feel it." The student thought that meant him, so he reached his ungloved hand into the patient's open chest. Shocked at this break into his sterile field, Dr. "O" followed the hand to the student. He didn't have to say a word. The embarrassed student quickly removed his hand.

If Dr. "O" ever saw med students downtown or anywhere, it didn't matter what celebrity he was with, he would always stop and talk to the students. It's no wonder that he was so loved and appreciated. He was one of the first to recognize the dangers of smoking. He used to say, "One package of cigarettes a day for twenty years—cancer of the lung." At that time 85% of our class smoked, and now I would say less than 5% of us do. We learned our lessons well. I graduated in 1955 as an MD. After New Orleans, I went to Mobile, Alabama, for one year of internship and four years of training in general and thoracic surgery

Chapter Seven
Mobile, Alabama,
Internship and Residency

My first year in Mobile started out as a living hell. I had a wife and two kids to support, and very little money. The only place I could find to live in was a place called "Birdville," and believe me, it was for the birds! It was the worst place I've ever lived in. The first few days we lived there, we had to sleep on the floor, and the roaches were so bad that they would fall off the ceiling at night, and fall on us as we tried to sleep. I think the place was a hangout for criminals and drug dealers. We did our best to clear out the roaches, but they won out, and after about three weeks of that, I had to move my family to better living conditions.

In the meantime, I had to have transportation back and forth from home and the hospital, so I went to a car dealer there who was selling cars at $100. What I bought wasn't much of a car, but it was transportation for a while. I went through three or four of these cars, and when they died, I would go back and get another $100 dollar car. One particular car that gave me some thrills was a Dodge Coupe. It looked pretty good, but it had a bad habit of losing its brakes. I would be driving home, when unexpectedly my brakes would go out. I had them repaired, but they would keep on failing, and when they did, I had to leave the road. I never hit anyone, but I was lucky. Finally I broke down and bought another junk heap.

Mobile, Alabama, in 1955 was a fairly typical southern city. There were four hospitals in the city: the Mobile Infirmary (strictly private), Providence Hospital (private), the sixth district Tuberculosis Hospital, (charity) and the Mobile General Hospital (charity). Internship and residency training was done at the two charity hospitals. It was no picnic to work as an intern or resident. My pay started at $50.00 per month as an intern. One week we worked 90 hours, and the second week we worked 120 hours. This lasted one year as an intern. No rest for the weary. In my fifth year at the Mobile General Hospital I was paid $150.00 per month as chief resident. In order to survive after internship, I took on the responsibility of medical director, worked as a nurse on obstetrics (delivered many babies) and worked in the emergency room. I also worked some weekends in Bayou la Batre to cover a general practitioner's practice. I had a wife and two kids to support, so I did whatever I had to do to survive.

As an intern, you rotate through the various departments of obstetrics and gynecology, internal medicine, urology, surgery, orthopedics, pediatrics, and emergency medicine. I worked all of the time. I would go into the hospital at seven a.m. on a Monday morning, work all day as a resident, take call that night as a resident (up all night), work Tuesday doing surgery, (seeing patients, etc.), and then work Tuesday night as the nurse on obstetrics. I had two hours off between five and seven before going to work in the obstetrics unit. The next morning, Wednesday, I would work all day as a resident doing surgery until five o'clock, and then go home and collapse. I did this for months on end, and they said that being a doctor was easy. Ha!

Traveling to Bayou la Batre was a nice break from the rat race at the hospital. An amusing incident happened to me one day while seeing patients there. A lady came in to see me about getting a shot for a cold, except that it wasn't for her, it was for her Rhesus monkey that she was carrying in her arms. I couldn't believe it, but she told me her doctor always treated the monkey and gave it a shot of penicillin. Since I was covering his practice, I was trapped, so I listened to the monkey's chest, looked at his throat, and gave it a shot. I felt like a fool, but Mama and monkey went away contented. I thought then, what extremes does a person have to go to in order to support his family?

A nice memory while I was there was being invited to a patient's home for a delicious dinner of chicken and oyster gumbo each weekend. I had previously done surgery on a member of this family, and they were just showing their appreciation. These were just good, down-to-earth folks, and I really appreciated them.

While on duty in the emergency room in Mobile, I saw a patient with a rapid heartbeat of 180 (paroxysmal tachycardia). This is very frightening to the patient and potentially dangerous. Conversion to normal sinus rhythm must be done. We use several methods to slow the heart. One is to press on the patient's eyeballs, which stimulates the vagus nerve and slows the heart. Another is to have the patient hold his breath, and while he does so, squeeze their upper chest to increase intrathoracic pressure. If these methods fail, an intravenous injection of digitalis usually will produce the desired result. After trying the first two procedures with no response, I started to give the patient an injection of digitalis. She said, "No doctor, you are not giving me a shot."

I said "Why not? I'm trying to slow your heart down."

She said, "Doctor, the last time I was given a shot, I got pregnant!"

I said, "You've got to be kidding; this shot will not get you pregnant." I persisted, gave her the injection.

When I finished, she said, "Okay, when I has this baby, I'm bringing it back to you." I told her it wasn't this shot that got her pregnant; it was that other shot in the dark that did it.

Another amusing story was when a grandmother brought her 15-year-old granddaughter into the emergency room for an examination. She had been nauseated and was vomiting, so granny was trying to help her. After my examination, I found that she was pregnant and was having morning sickness. When I told Granny, she said, "How can that be? She's not even married." I told her that you don't have to be married to get pregnant. With a puzzled look on her face, she said "Well, she does sleep in the same bed with my son and his wife. Do you think she could have been splashed?" This was a difficult situation to explain.

Mobile General's emergency room was not always a pleasant place to practice. There was always an overabundance of patients to see with a variety of problems: simple lacerations, respiratory infections, women in labor, heart attacks, gunshot wounds, stab wounds, auto accident victims, and other problems. The medical staff did its best to give proper care and treat the patients with respect, but this was not always possible. One night I was awakened at two a.m. to take care of a patient in the ER. He was a well-dressed, intelligent, and apparently well-respected member of the community. He had a three-inch laceration of his hand where he had tried to punch someone through a car window. He came to the general hospital because he was ashamed and afraid of being recognized if he went to the Mobile Infirmary, and that treatment there could hurt his reputation. His attitude was hostile, and his language abusive. He felt that he was above being treated in the charity hospital by residents. I prepared to suture his wound, and he became even more abusive, but in spite of this, I started to suture his wound. He continued cursing me, and that did it! I told the nurse to get an ambulance and transfer him to the Mobile Infirmary. I had taken all of the crap that I was willing to take from him. Let him go get taken care of at the infirmary, and be embarrassed. I had enough of his mouth at two a.m.

One night one of the night fighters came to the ER with a small laceration, and because everyone was busy, he was asked by the nurse to wait his turn. He continued to be abusive to the nurse, and I went out to try to reason with him. With that, he pulled out a knife and came after me. Fortunately for me, two policemen were there and saw what happened. They said, "Don't worry, Doc; we'll take care of him, and they took him out to the street. They took care of him all right. When he came back, instead of one laceration to suture, I had three or four. Blackjacks are very effective, and he was a whipped puppy. From then on, he was very polite and subdued. I'll bet he never pulled a knife on another doctor. I sewed up his lacerations and sent him home.

Sometimes patients arriving in the ER are unruly and totally out of control. In these cases, we have to subdue the patient to keep him from hurting himself or someone else. We then often give them a sedative so that we could treat them. When this happens, the doctors and nurses on duty all help to try to control the patient. One night while wrestling with a patient, he got out of our grasp, and he got his head around to my back and bit me. He almost bit a chunk the size of his mouth out of my back. I carried the scar of his teeth marks on my back for months.

We worked long hours and got little sleep, so we slept when we could. One night while on the OB service, my phone rang, and I woke up in the hospital lobby. I wondered what I was doing there, and then it dawned on me that maybe they had called me to deliver a baby. I then went to the delivery room that was on the second floor, and the attendants hollered at me to hurry, that she was ready. I scrubbed and delivered the baby while still half asleep.

While working as a nurse on OB (in my spare time—ha!) I worked with an elderly Negro aide that had worked there for years. She was wonderful to me and had probably delivered more babies than any doctor in training at that hospital. She knew the long hours that I had to work, and she felt sorry for me. She would tell me to take a nap, and then she would call me when I was needed for a delivery. I needed that, since this was my second night with no sleep. One night, some of my friends knew that I was working as the nurse on OB for extra money, and they decided to play a trick on me. I was catching a nap when someone slammed open the doors to the delivery, and in came a cart with what I thought was a screaming pregnant woman under a sheet. I rushed out only to see that it was one of my fellow doctors rattling my cage. When I saw that, I put on a rectal glove and told him that I was going to do a rectal exam on him, and with that, he took off laughing.

Before too many months, I realized that my calling was in the department of surgery, where I spent a lot of time. The training at Mobile General Hospital was great. It prepared me well for later years when I was the only board-certified surgeon between Pensacola, Montgomery, and Panama City for 16 years.

Medicine and medical practice have changed dramatically since I arrived in Mobile in 1955. I'll recall many cases and practices from that era and compare them later to the many marvels of medicine and surgery available today. These are all true stories, and I'm pleased to have played a part in this short episode in history. Some are funny, some serious, but all patients were treated with respect. They were all human beings, and we were there to help them in their time of need. This was back in the days when patients were separated into "white" and "colored" male and female wards. There was a very active emergency room and out-patient service. We had three operating rooms and two delivery rooms, and they stayed very busy.

Mobile General Hospital was an old group of buildings. Some of them dated back to the Civil War. On occasion there would be a malfunction, and some of the things that we take for granted would break down (like air conditioning). Trying to do surgery in the heat of summer without air conditioning was no fun. On rare occasions and emergencies we had to do just that. Trying to keep a sterile field when you have on a hot gown and gloves and are sweating is a challenge. None of the clinics were air conditioned, and we used fans to circulate the air. When crowded, the odor was almost overwhelming. The worst place in summer was the cystoscopy room. There were no windows, and the smell of urine was intense. Imagine doing a cystoscopic procedure with your nose close to a patient's crotch with those conditions. That was no fun, but we survived.

Interns on each service followed residents around and were shown procedures, and then allowed to do the procedure themselves under supervision. Early on I had an early experience while I was on the orthopedic service. A patient in the emergency room had a colles fracture. This is a fracture of the of the distal (forearm), close to the hand. It is a displaced fracture, and the resident was going to show me how to reduce it (fix it). He did this, applied a cast, and sent the patient home. Five weeks later I saw him in the outpatient clinic.

It was his patient, but I got an x-ray, and the fracture had slipped and was displaced. It had healed, but he had a deformed arm. It was embarrassing to see it, but he wanted no more treatment from the doctor that had set it. After that I saw him in passing at places away from the hospital, and he would wave at me with that crooked arm— I kept telling him I didn't set it, but he didn't care. He called me his doctor as I tried to hide my embarrassment.

At that time polio was a common disease. At Charity Hospital in New Orleans there was a separate building for polio patients of all ages. This was before the discovery of the vaccine. We had adult patients in Mobile using iron lungs. It was very sad. It was a milestone in medicine when Dr. Jonas Salk discovered the polio vaccine. What a great step forward! Polio is now rare.

Back then if a patient had renal (kidney) shutdown for any reason, there was no such thing as kidney dialysis. Sometimes renal shutdown was for advanced kidney disease; sometimes it was for ingestion of toxins or drugs. We saved some patients by doing a very crude peritoneal dialysis. We ran ringers solution into the peritoneal (abdominal) cavity from one side and drained it out the other side. It was very primitive but it was all that we had. We were able to help some patients but not all. Today we have kidney dialysis—what an improvement!

The Charity Hospital system worked very well at that time in Mobile, Alabama. The Catholic sisters of Charity ran the hospital. Medical care was administered by the hospital staff, consisting of private physicians volunteering their time on each service for the sole purpose of teaching, the medical director, and the intern and resident staff. There were staff meetings, grand rounds, and consultation with private physicians on patient care, case presentations, and individual instruction. The system worked very well, and patient care was excellent. The consulting staff (private physicians) provided guidance on how to best care for the patients. The medical staff, eager to learn and impress their tutors, would strive to provide the best of care to patients which would help them recover rapidly from their illnesses or surgery. No patient was ever turned away or refused care. The county paid for the care of these indigent patients.

One of the reasons I chose Mobile General Hospital for my internship was because the volume of patients seen there would provide excellent experience and training to a new physician. There was a good teaching program, and the interns and residents would receive good hands-on experience and supervision. I had no idea when I went there that I would end up specializing in surgery. I just took it one year at a time. When I went there, acceptable resident surgical training was either at a hospital that provided four years of specializing in surgery, or at a hospital that provided three years of specialized training and then two years of apprenticeship with a board-qualified surgeon.

At the time, Mobile had only a three-year program, but our chief of surgery, Dr. James Donald, wanted the hospital to qualify for a four-year program. I was delighted, because if we were successful and were qualified and accepted, I would be the first four-year surgical resident at that hospital. That meant that on completion of my training, I would then be board eligible and would not have to train with a preceptor. The only problem was that I was under the gun and had to survive the scrutiny of the inspectors from the American College of Surgeons, the American Board of Surgery, the American Hospital Association, and others. Since I was chief resident, they not only checked the hospital facility, but they checked me. They checked all of the cases I had operated on since arriving at that hospital and the results. The hospital and I passed with flying colors, and we were then formally approved for a four-year residency program in general surgery.

While there, Dr. James Donald instituted a program open to all of the surgical residents in the state of Alabama. He set up a competition amongst the residents to write a paper, and the winner would have the privilege of presenting it to the annual meeting of the Alabama chapter of the American College of Surgeons. This meant that all expenses were paid for four days: quite a treat for a poor resident. I won the contest and presented the paper to the group at their meeting at Point Clear, Alabama. The contest is still being held, and the James Donald Award is still an active part of the annual meeting to this day. He was a good surgeon with a lot of vision and compassion. He taught me a lot. I was chief resident under his leadership and instruction for two and a half years.

The paper that I presented at that meeting was about a four-pound-thirteen-ounce twin delivered at home by a midwife. The baby came into the hospital 16 days old severely dehydrated due to persistent vomiting after each feeding. The child was started on intravenous fluids, and further evaluation showed that the child had a duodenal atresia (congenital blockage of the first part of the small bowel). This is a rare occurrence, with the incidence being once in every 40,000 births. The next day, after hydration and correction of electrolytes, he was taken to surgery, where a duodenal atresia was found, and the obstruction was repaired by duodeno jejunostomy (small bowel to small bowel, bypassing the obstruction). His post operative course was uneventful, as he was able to eat normally and gain weight. He was discharged after twenty days weighing six pounds, six ounces. Follow up six months later revealed that he weighed more than his twin brother and was doing well. This case was unusual and interesting because prior to this, in searching the medical literature, no infant with duodenal atresia had ever lived longer than 12 days. This baby came in to the hospital 16 days after birth and survived. Tough kid!

Chapter Eight
Early Days of Medicare

Before the days of Medicare, there were no government health-care programs. After Medicare, everything changed. Patients who qualified for Medicare then became private patients, and consulting doctors who had previously donated their services by teaching, were now being paid by Medicare. This was the first step in government intervention in medicine, and while it helped many people, in this case it was detrimental to the teaching program. Whereas previously, participating physicians on the hospital staff were honored by being a part of the teaching staff and were also proud of passing their knowledge on to these young physicians thirsting for knowledge, now it was more of a business. They got paid for their services. Another negative side effect was that some cases that were available for teaching (with supervision) were now taken over by staff physicians, who did their own surgery, and this dried up many of the cases that were available for interns and residents in training. This lessened the experience for the trainees, and many doctors entered private practice with less knowledge and skill than if they had been exposed to more cases and responsibility in their training.

Today, there is much talk about the health care crisis in our country. Everyone has his own ideas. Here are mine. Rather than having the government spend billions on a grandiose scheme to pay for everyone's health care, why not have a plan (with modifications) to have a government-sponsored health-care program to either purchase private hospitals, or build a system of hospitals expressly for taking care of patients who are indigent or have no health-care insurance. This would solve the problem of taking care of the segment of the population that cannot afford health care. It would be expensive, but not nearly as expensive as providing health care for every US citizen. Most people can afford to buy their own health insurance. And most people do not want a government handout. By the government not having to pay healthcare costs for all citizens it could more easily afford these hospitals. Now, to help those buying their own health care, give them a tax write off, or tax credit to help off set their costs. (Still a lot less cost to the government than providing health care to all.) These hospitals can be used as teaching hospitals, with private physicians honored to be part of a teaching staff. Give them tax breaks for their participation. This plan would drive liberals crazy because the government would spend less money!

Chapter Nine
Interesting Cases

During my five years spent in training, I would like to recall some of the interesting cases I took care of at the hospital. The general hospital and its staff had an overabundance of cases of trauma. I was a junior resident for one and one half years and chief resident for two and a half years. I personally saw and treated these people. We, as a staff were proud to say that even with very serious gunshot wounds, if they made it to the hospital most of them survived.

Five years at the Mobile General Hospital exposed me to a variety of experiences in the various surgical specialties. We trained in general and thoracic surgery, orthopedics, obstetrics gynecology, urology, and ENT surgery.

A rare complication in a newborn child is a spontaneous rupture of the esophagus (the swallowing tube between the mouth and the stomach). I had the good fortune of being able to successfully repair one of these in a female newborn child. At that time, fewer than 200 cases of rupture of the esophagus had been reported in the medical literature. Only 35% of these lived 24 hours without corrective surgery. This child came in to the hospital shortly after birth with obvious respiratory distress, and x-rays revealed a tension pneumothorax (air in the chest outside of the lung compressing the lung). Exploration of the right chest cavity revealed air and about 200 ccs. of milk inside the space, as a consequence of the parent feeding the child right after birth. A one-cm. perforation was identified in the mid portion of the esophagus that was the source of the leak. The leak was repaired, the chest cavity cleaned out, chest tubes were inserted for drainage, and the patient was then sent to the recovery room. Post operatively, the child recovered uneventfully and was sent home. The paper reporting this unusual case was published in the medical literature, in the *Journal of Pediatrics* in August of 1959.

One day, a tall woman with a very large abdomen came into the emergency room. She was in obvious discomfort due to an extremely large and protruding abdomen. The lady thought she might be pregnant, but she recalled having this large abdomen for over a year. Examination revealed no sign of pregnancy; instead it appeared that she had a large collection of fluid in the abdomen. Could this be ascites (fluid loose in the abdomen), or was this a very large ovarian cyst? After a complete evaluation, we still had no answer, so I took her to surgery, and at exploration, I found an 85-pound ovarian cyst growing in the abdominal cavity. Careful dissection and removal of its blood supply then allowed me to free it from the surrounding abdominal contents. My next problem was to move it and still keep the operative field sterile. I couldn't lift it, so we pulled a table with sterile sheets on it next to the operating table. With that, I was able to roll the large cyst, intact, over to the table, while freeing it up from the surrounding tissues. It was then sent to pathology, and it was determined to be benign. The cyst had been there so long that her rib cage had actually flared out to conform to the shape of the cyst. I have never seen an ovarian cyst so large. The excess skin was removed, and the abdomen was closed. She recovered uneventfully, and left the hospital in about eight days, 85 pounds lighter.

I was being trained in general and thoracic surgery, but at times we had to take care of whatever problem that came along. One of these cases involved a male patient who came into the emergency room with a head injury after an automobile accident. He was semiconscious, and I determined that he had a subdural hematoma (collection of blood between the brain and the skull). If this situation was allowed to progress untreated, pressure on the brain would cause unconsciousness and death.

I'm not a neurosurgeon, so I called one of the only two neurosurgeons practicing in the city of Mobile, and described the patient's symptoms. The patient's condition was getting worse, and the neurosurgeon agreed that he needed his skull opened and the bleeding stopped. The only problem was that he and the other neurosurgeon were in surgery at another hospital, and they couldn't leave. What a revolting development this was, so I said, "What do I do now?"

He said, "Go ahead and crack his skull, or he'll die." He jokingly said, "Just don't be a plunger."

Very funny! I said, "Hell, I'm not a neurosurgeon!"

So he said, "You've watched me do it a dozen times; go ahead."

So I did. The patient was unconscious by then, so I deadened his scalp with a local anesthetic and prepared to open his skull. The tool used in those days to drill through the bone looked like an old-fashioned brace and bit used by carpenters doing woodwork. I very carefully and very nervously proceeded to drill into his skull. After I drilled through the bone, I opened the dura, and identified the source of the arterial bleeding. I then stopped the bleeding, and sucked out the blood that had collected on his brain. At that time, the patient began to wake up on the table, and he had to be restrained while I closed the incision. He did well, and I showed him off as my one and only neurosurgical case on weekly rounds with our staff. I was proud of him, and the staff kidded me and asked when was I going to send him home. "I said I'm so proud of him that I may just adopt him."

As I said earlier, we sometimes were called on to do things relegated to other specialties. As a resident, I worked as a nurse on obstetrics (for extra money) and also was in charge of the Ob/Gyn service. As such, I delivered many babies and performed many cesarean sections. One c-section that I recall was unusual and a departure from the routine. At that time, one of my residents was taking care of a patient in labor and at term. She had delivered one child from below, and the next by section. He asked if he could deliver this baby from below, and I said, "No way."

In those days, the old classical caesarean section was commonly being used (up and down vertical incision) and the incidence of uterine rupture was high when a patient went into labor. Our motto was, "Once a section, always a section," so I directed him to take her to the operating room. The operating room was ready, and the resident excitedly called me into the operating room to see the patient. When I did, her abdomen was no longer symmetrical and round, it had a hump in it like a camel's back. Feeling the abdomen revealed a soft, "squishy" feel. I immediately knew that she had a ruptured uterus, and said "Put her to sleep; I don't have time to scrub." I put on a gown and gloves and was in her abdomen in two to three minutes. The uterus had ruptured, and the full-term baby was out of the uterus and lying free in the abdominal cavity. I removed the baby, tied off the umbilical cord, and we had a live baby. Because of the torn uterus and the bleeding I went ahead and did a hysterectomy at the same time. It was very exciting. We ended up with a live baby and a live mother; there was no time for indecision. I sometimes wonder, though, in today's litigious society how much I would have been sued for if I had lost the baby or the mother in that emergency.

The pharmacy at the hospital was across the hall from the operating room. One day, one of the pharmacists, a very sweet young girl, collapsed while working. Examination revealed a very tender abdomen, and needle tap of the abdomen revealed the presence of blood. She was in shock, and we rushed her to the operating room, suspecting that she had ruptured an ectopic pregnancy (pregnancy in a fallopian tube). When I opened the belly, sure enough, she was bleeding profusely from a pregnancy in one of her fallopian tubes that had ruptured. I removed the tube and ovary, controlled the bleeding, and sent her to the recovery room. She recovered nicely and was discharged in a few days to recover at home.

Gunshot wounds were very common in Mobile, Alabama, especially on Saturday nights. It was not unusual for the emergency room staff to take care of at least two or three of these during one night. Not all of them had to go to surgery. Some with superficial wounds were treated and released. One night, two males showed up, each with a single gunshot to the abdomen and both needed surgery. The problem was that we had only one operating room and crew available, and only me with enough training under my belt to do the surgery. Which one goes to surgery first? I chose the one with the lowest blood pressure first, assuming that he had lost the most blood. In retrospect it was a good decision. His injury was two holes in the stomach, perforation of the diaphragm, and severe damage to the spleen. I performed a splenectomy, repaired the holes in the stomach and diaphragm, and he was then sent to the recovery room and recovered nicely.

The operating room was then quickly cleaned up and readied for the next warrior, while I took a quick nap. This second patient was then taken to the operating room, and I then explored his abdomen. He had similar injuries, with perforations of the stomach, duodenum, transverse colon, liver, and spleen. I repaired the perforations, removed the spleen, and then sent him to recovery. Both patients recovered without any complications, and were sent home in a week. Another routine exiting evening on surgical call.

Another interesting story is about two patients who came into the emergency room at different times, but had similar circumstances and similar injuries. It seems that both of these individuals were in the wrong place at the wrong time, and suffered the consequences. In each case it was a male making love to someone else's wife, when the irate husband walked in on them from behind, while the action was going on. The irate spouse pulled out a gun, and shot the lover from behind. (We used to say that he caught him on the rise.) The bullet penetrated the buttocks, and entered the abdomen. In each case, I had to explore the abdomen to trace the path of the bullet and repair the injuries. The bullet passed through muscle, colon, small bowel, stomach, and diaphragm. The various perforations were closed, and in each case the embarrassed patients recovered and left the hospital to fight again, hopefully a little bit smarter than when they came into the hospital. It was unusual to see two patients with similar injuries caught in the same embarrassing position.

One day while on call in the hospital, I was called on to see a patient in the emergency room who had been shot in the chest. He was in shock and had a wound of entry on the left side of the chest above the heart, and a cracked rib on the right side of the chest. It appeared from our studies that this man had a through-and-through gunshot wound of the heart. I could not believe that this man was still alive after sustaining a gunshot wound of the heart with a .38-caliber bullet. As chief resident, I dutifully called our staff doctor, described his condition, as a gunshot of the heart, and asked his permission to operate (as if there was any question).

His answer was, "Have you been drinking?"

I said no, but I had to take this man to surgery right away. Our staff was used to emergencies, so we wasted no time getting everything ready.

This was in the days before open-heart surgery, and we didn't even have a sternum-splitting knife that is used today routinely to get into the chest. I chose to open his chest transversely, right to left, and open it up like a car hood so that I would be able to visualize the heart. We had to make do with whatever we had. I gathered my residents, and we started IVs in each arm and each leg, contemplating excessive blood loss, which we had, when I opened the chest. When I did this, all hell broke loose. Blood went everywhere, and I was soaked in blood from the waist down. My residents started pumping blood. There was no heart lung machine, and all I had for anesthesia was an excellent nurse anesthetist. This case was so unusual that we wrote it up in the *American Journal of Surgery*, Volume 97, March 1959, and I'll now reprint the original article as it was written.

Perforating Wound of Two Chambers of the Heart with Survival
J. Richard Moore M.D. and Eugene R. Celano, M.D. Mobile, Alabama.

Many cases of penetrating wounds of the heart with successful repair have been reported in the recent literature. The present case is unusual in that it involved a through-and-through perforation through two chambers of the heart. Review of the current literature does not disclose any other such cases in which the patient survived.

Case Report

On August 8, 1957, a thirty-three-year-old Negro man entered the emergency room of the county hospital, Mobile, Alabama, with a gunshot wound of the left chest approximately three cms. below the left nipple. The injury had occurred shortly before admission. The patient was irrational and there was a strong alcoholic odor to his breath; the skin was cold and clammy. Blood pressure was 70/58 mm.hg., pulse 110, and respirations 30. Breath sounds were decreased to the left side of the chest. A hematoma was noted with evidence of a fractured sixth rib in the mid axillary line on the right side. There was no wound of exit. On examination of the heart, no murmurs were heard, sounds were decreased in intensity and there was a sinus tachycardia. The extremities had equal pulsations bilaterally and there was no venous distention. A presumptive diagnosis of gunshot wound of the heart was made, and the patient was given intravenous glucose while blood was obtained for typing and cross matching. The pericardium was aspirated through the chest and 20 ccs. of blood was removed from the pericardial cavity. The heart sounds improved somewhat and blood pressure rose to 90/60 mm.hg. While the operating room was being prepared a blood transfusion was begun through a no. 15 polyethylene catheter into the left saphenous vein. Portable chest x-ray showed cardiac enlargement with increased density of the entire right lung field with a metallic foreign body lying adjacent to the right sixth rib in the mid-axillary line. The patient was placed under general endotracheal anesthesia and prepared for exploratory thoracotomy. This was approximately two hours after admission to the emergency room. Blood pressure at this time was 110/80 mm.hg.

With the patient in the supine position the right chest was opened rapidly through the sixth intercostal space from the mid axillary line to the sternal border. Upon entering the pleural space approximately 1500 ccs. of blood was found in the right chest. Perforation was noted in the pericardium that was bleeding copiously. One finger was inserted through the pericardial opening and a perforation in the right atrium was discovered; tamponade was performed. The pericardial sac was opened transversely while this bleeding point was temporarily arrested. The sternum was transected and the incision made through the left sixth intercostal space. The pericardial opening was extended transversely across the midline exposing the left side of the heart. An additional smaller perforation was found .5 cm. to the left of the anterior descending branch of the left coronary artery. This perforation was rapidly closed with interrupted sutures of no. 5-0 black silk, care being taken not to include the anterior descending branch of the left coronary artery. At this point, the blood pressure dropped to zero and cardiac standstill occurred. Cardiac massage was initiated with one finger still occluding the opening in the right atrium. Sinus rhythm returned; however, due to marked hypotension, a levophed drip was started which rapidly produced a systolic pressure of over 100 mm.hg. The perforation of the right atrium was closed with no. 3-0 black silk suture. During this suturing cardiac standstill occurred three more times; cardiac massage was performed and sinus rhythm returned. Following closure of both perforations, the blood pressure began to rise and levophed drip was discontinued. Three thousand cubic centimers of blood was given during the operative procedure. Anesthesia was minimal with the lungs being aerated almost entirely with oxygen. The pericardium was left open. The heart was slightly dilated with a sinus tachycardia of 110; blood pressure was 110/80 mm.hg. The chest was closed with water trap suction draining the pleural space. The patient's immediate postoperative condition was

LOOKING BACK

highly satisfactory, and in the recovery room he responded rapidly and was able to answer questions within thirty minutes after leaving the operating room.

The postoperative course was entirely uneventful except for temperature elevation ranging from 98° to 101°F for a nine-day period. The patient was treated with routine supportive care with prophylactic penicillin and tetracycline. Serial electrocardiograms revealed only pericarditis. No murmurs were heard at any time and he had a normal sinus rhythm. Serial chest films reveal pleural reaction and slight cardiac enlargement. The patient left the hospital on the sixteenth postoperative day apparently well. A communication from him some three months later advised that he had returned to full manual labor with no apparent disability.

The bullet recovered from the right chest cavity was proved to be a .38 caliber. The presumed course of the bullet was through the ventricular surface at the left of the interventricular septum with perforation of the right ventricle. The bullet apparently proceeded through the right tricuspid valve while it was open and emerged through the wall of the right atrium approximately one cm. anterior to the level of the inferior vena cava. It is postulated that fatal hemorrhage did not occur immediately because of a tamponading of the pericardial sac against the opening of the right atrium, and the ventricular opening bled very little because of the tangential path of the bullet through the heavy muscular fibers of the interventricular septum.

During the excitement of the cardiac massages, my staff man walked in and said he couldn't believe it, but if this guy made it he would buy everyone in the operating room the biggest steak that Constantine's could prepare. I said, "You're on," and later he was good to his word and paid off. He took about eight of us to a fabulous dinner.

The next day, the patient was sitting up in bed in the recovery room reading the police gazette. Unbelievable! Twenty-five or thirty years later I received a call from my staff man at the time who told me that our patient was now on social security.

On Sept 18,1957, I received a letter from him, and this is what he wrote, and as he wrote it (names have been changed).

Dear Dr. Egene just a few line to let you here from me, I am well and hope you are keeping the good work up. Dr. I didn't get here until Sunday night so I am going to a doctor today but I am doing fine and by the help of you and God I will make it. I just fiel a little num cross the chest. I just that wont last loing so Dr I naver will forget what you and God done for me as long as I live. So I will close my letter but not my heart and say may the good Lord help you keep up the good work. Until we meet agin good by and good luck

Form Zachariah Davis

One month later, I received the following note from his parents.

Dr Eugene jast line to let you her from us we are fine and hope you is the same Dr Zachariah is fine thank God and you.

I may bring him to see some time in December if God say so I close my letter from Mrs Hart and Mr Hart and Zach with all ther loves

This brought tears to my eyes, but this is what makes it all worthwhile. A year or so later, I had a patient with the same type of injury, but this was with a .22 caliber bullet so it wasn't nearly as dramatic. He, too, survived but I didn't put it in a medical journal for fear that they would question my honesty.

LOOKING BACK

In Mobile, we took pride in the care that we gave to patients. We used to say that if they arrived at the hospital alive after a gunshot wound, that we could save all of them. Unfortunately, that was not always the case, and we would lose one every now and then.

One case I recall was on a night when one of the local tough guys, known as Tiger, came into the emergency room with multiple gun shot wounds from a .38-caliber pistol. This was a well-known warrior who was well respected and feared in the black community. Someone finally got to him and gunned him down. As soon as he arrived at the hospital we went to work on him. He was in shock from the blood loss, and we transfused him with O-negative blood. His injuries were very serious. In a short time we could see that we were not making any progress, and we took him to surgery to try to save him. Upon opening his abdomen it was obvious that his blood loss was so profuse that we could not keep up unless we were able to control the major cause of his bleeding. It was too late, and we lost Tiger on the operating table. We did our best, but the severity of his injuries and the time it took to get him to the hospital were more than we were able to overcome. We were all upset, but we did the best that we could, and realized that you just cannot save them all.

One of the problems a surgeon will encounter in his career is the occurrence of cardiac arrest. This complication can occur for various reasons, among them, anoxia, anesthesia, drug reaction, allergy, blood loss, and heart attack. Cardiac arrest or sudden stoppage of the heart is an immediate emergency, and when this happens immediate action is required, or the patient dies. Today if the heart goes into ventricular fibrillation, a defibrillator, using electric paddles and electric shock can usually convert the fibrillating heart to a regular sinus rhythm. In those days, if the action of the heart totally stopped the only option we had was to open the chest, and manually massage the heart to try to get it to beat on its own.

During my residency, on several occasions I was put in the position of having to open the chest and massage the heart to try to restore its normal beat. This is not always successful, depending on the cause of the arrest, but we were fortunate enough to save several lives with our efforts. When this happens, time is the enemy, and no time can be wasted. Sterlity is usually compromised, but the chest has to be opened immediately. If there is no endotracheal tube in place, it must be immediately inserted, and 100 % oxygen given. One case that I specifically remember was a four-to-five-year-old boy who arrested while having surgery. We immediately stopped the surgery and opened the chest. Pure oxygen was given, and his heartbeat returned within a few minutes of starting massage. His heartbeat returned to a normal sinus rhythm. The chest was closed, and he was sent to intensive care to be monitored. He was placed on antibiotics and recovered with no other problems. I cannot recall the reason for the arrest, but it turned out that he was one of the lucky ones.

I saw a bizarre situation in the emergency room one night. I was called to see a patient who had been shot in the head. When I examined him, he had a wound of entry on one side of his head, and a bullet was palpated on the other side of his head. It appeared that he had sustained a through-and-through gunshot of the head. He was alert, had no neurological signs of brain injury, and no weakness in any of his extremities. I said, "How can this be?" It looked like he had sustained a through-and-through gunshot of the head, but had no symptoms other than a headache. Puzzled, I got an x-ray of his skull, and bullet fragments were seen from the wound of entry going under the scalp, over the top, but above the skull, going over to the other side, where the bullet fragment was lodged. The bullet never entered the skull, and it had left a path between the skull and the scalp. I removed the bullet fragment, put him on antibiotics, and kept him in the hospital for observation. He recovered with no problems and was sent home. I've heard of hard heads, but this was ridiculous. He was a very lucky guy to be shot in the head and have no complications.

A patient I saw in the emergency room in Mobile came in with a painful problem with his penis. He had never been circumcised, and he was now in his eighties. The foreskin on the penis was swollen, and stuck behind the head of the penis, causing considerable discomfort. I was able to anesthetize the area, and then slip the foreskin back over the head of the penis into its original area, and this gave him immediate relief. Someone asked how this happened, and he replied that he was having sexual intercourse. He was then asked, "How long does this sex thing go on?"

He said, "I don't know. You'll have to ask someone older than me."

Some of my training was done at the Sixth District Tuberculosis Hospital in Mobile. While there we saw and evaluated patients in various stages of tuberculosis. We really had to be careful there, since some of the patients were angry because they had the disease, and they would cough in the face of the examiner. They were supposed to wear masks, but they often removed them. In that hospital, we did surgery on patients who did not respond to anti-TB therapy. A lung infected with tuberculosis is very difficult to operate on because of the scarring associated with the disease. To do surgery on these lungs, you really have to know what you are doing. While there, I had the privilege and honor of working with an excellent surgeon, Earnest Debakey. He is the brother of the Houston heart surgeon, Michael Debakey. I learned a lot from him. His technique was so good that he made even the hardest cases look easy.

Chapter Ten
Where to Practice

Five years at the Mobile General Hospital exposed me to a variety of experiences in the various surgical specialties. I performed, taught, or participated in over 1500 surgical cases. My last two and a half years as chief resident were spent in surgery on more complicated cases as well as teaching interns and residents. After all of this, I was well prepared for what lay ahead of me as the only surgeon in a small town.

Prior to the completion of my residency, a fellow doctor and I traveled all over the whole state of Florida looking for a place to settle down and practice medicine. On the way back to Mobile, we stopped at Eglin AFB golf course for lunch. We both had a hamburger and one beer. When we left to go back home, we went by way of Highway 98. I was driving a 1956 Cadillac Eldorado, and my friend asked me how fast the car would go. I told him I had never tried it so I didn't know. So he said, "Try it." There was no traffic on the road, so I opened it up through Navarre, Florida. At that time there was no population in that area, so I opened it up until I got to 115 miles per hour and then I slowed it down. About that time a highway patrolman caught me with lights flashing and pulled me down. This was a big man that looked like Matt Dillon, and he was not too happy. When my friend got out of the car, he stumbled, and the officer then said, "Oh! So you've been drinking, too!"

We told him that we only had one beer with lunch, but I didn't convince him, so he instructed me to follow him to Milton, the county seat of Santa Rosa County. It was about thirty-five miles away, and I told him that I didn't have enough gas to get there. He reluctantly agreed to let me stop and get gas before going on to the courthouse. Once we got there, they booked me, and told me that I was allowed one phone call before locking me up. I made one call. The line was busy, and the clerk then said, "Okay, that's it; you're going to jail," and away I went.

Between my friend and me we didn't have enough money to make bail, but my friend's mother lived in Pensacola, and later that night she drove up and bailed me out. Before she arrived, they put me in a cell with four other prisoners. I decided then and there that I was going to tell them that I had killed somebody, and maybe they would leave me alone. They turned out to be friendly, and offered me some of the beans that they were eating. The urinal was about three feet away from the food, and I didn't have much of an appetite. About midnight, my friend's mother arrived with the bail (God bless her), and I was released to go home. I didn't test the car again.

Chapter Eleven
Fort Walton Beach:
The Early Days

Fort Walton Beach was a small, northwest Florida town when I arrived in July 1960. The population of the entire county was approximately 60,000. This included Crestview (the county seat), Niceville, Valparaiso, Eglin Air Force Base, and Fort Walton Beach. A good number of the population was military and eligible for medical care at Elgin Air Force Base hospital. There were ten physicians when I arrived. One practiced obstetrics and gynecology, one was a pediatrician, and there were eight general practitioners. I met with Jerry Melvin, who was with the Chamber of Commerce. (He later became a Florida state representative.) He convinced me to come to the area. I told him at the time that I had specialized in surgery, and that the area was too small for a surgeon, and that I didn't want to end up doing general practice. He told me that the city council was going to vote imminently to increase the hospital from twenty-five beds to fifty beds. He said the area was growing rapidly (a true salesman). I told him that I would return, and if this was going to happen, that I would consider opening a practice of surgery in the area.

When I returned, the expansion had been approved, and I decided to stay and open up a practice in surgery. Jerry Melvin and I celebrated over a cup of coffee at staff's restaurant. This made me the only board-eligible (and later board-certified) surgeon in an area of one hundred miles between Pensacola and Panama City, and about one hundred and fifty miles to Montgomery, Alabama. There wasn't much population, and I felt like a true country surgeon. I was the only board-certified surgeon in this area for the next sixteen years, when another board eligible surgeon arrived in town. He was a welcome addition to the community.

In those days, in order to be eligible to take the exams from the American Board of Surgery, an applicant had two options. One option was to take three years of approved residency, followed by two years of apprenticeship with an approved board certified surgeon in an active surgical practice. The other was to take four years of training in an approved residency program to be eligible to take the boards.

As I had mentioned previously, Mobile General Hospital had been approved for the full four-year program, so that when I finished my residency program, I was eligible to take the boards, which consisted of both oral and written exams. These exams were given with one day dedicated to oral and one day to written exams. This was no easy task, since the exams covered all aspects of general surgery, and when completed, you would be considered a fully trained and qualified surgeon. Completion is considered quite an accomplishment, and every surgeon is proud of and happy to hang the certificate of board certification on his office wall.

In the oral exams there is a lot of pressure on the applicant. You have to face three or four examiners in each sub-specialty of surgery (all experts in their field), and you are questioned at length as to your knowledge in the various fields of surgery. Prior to taking the exams, I spent a week in Chicago in a refresher course, so I knew the material very well and passed on my first try. I was very pleased to be able to achieve this goal.

Not all of the physicians on the staff of the hospital in Fort Walton Beach welcomed me with open arms. One of the docs that I talked to was a general practitioner, and apparently was doing a lot of surgery at that hospital. When I went to see him, I introduced myself and explained to him that I was a trained surgeon and considering a move to Fort Walton Beach to start my practice. He looked at me in all seriousness and said, "We don't need a surgeon here. I do all of the surgery that is done in this community."

I said "Thank you very much, and I'll see you later." It turned out that later we were to become the best of friends.

Another of my first encounters with the medical staff was with one of the older general practitioners. I met him at the hospital and introduced myself as a young surgeon considering coming to town to practice. He looked at me and said, "I hope you're a pro, we have enough amateurs already."

I looked him straight in the eyes, pointed to my chest, and said "I'm a pro." Cocky little devil wasn't I? Later I earned his respect, we became good friends, and I performed surgery on many of his patients, including a radical mastectomy on his wife.

When I arrived, I rented an office across the street from the hospital, but I had no furniture or equipment to go in it. I had ordered these items well in advance of my arrival, but the shipment was lost en route, and I had to reorder. There I was, broke, with a wife and three kids, a newly rented office, and no way to start a practice. What a revolting development this was. Fortunately an angel, who did general practice in Crestview, thirty miles away, came to my rescue. He offered to let me practice out of his office for free until my equipment arrived. This kept me going for three months until I could open my own office in Fort Walton Beach. In return, I helped him resolve several problems with some of his charity patients that needed surgery.

Starting a practice of surgery is never easy anywhere, but it is especially difficult in a small community. First of all, many patients had been seeing their own doctors for years, and were loyal and trusted them. In those days, major surgery was referred to surgeons in Pensacola, who had gotten referrals from these general practitioners for years and had earned their trust. This trend continued after my arrival in the community. A new doctor, especially a surgeon, has to prove himself capable in the eyes of the doctors practicing in the community, but also in the eyes of the residents of that community.

This takes time, but finally, as your work is highly scrutinized, if you are capable you earn the trust of the doctors and their patients, that is, if you don't screw up in the process. At that time, you begin to get referrals, and your practice slowly grows. Some doctors are forever skeptical and afraid that you will steal their patients, and they never come around to trusting you. I was very careful to send patients back to the referring physician after any surgical procedure so that this would never happen.

There was one doctor who, at every monthly medical meeting, would corner me and say, "I'm going to send you a patient."

I was polite, and would say, "Fine, I'll take good care of him and refer him back to you." It was almost a joke because I heard this story over a period of three years, and knew that this would never happen.

At a party one night, he came on to me with the same old line, and by then I had consumed a couple of drinks, so I told him, "Look, Max, I appreciate that, but I don't need or want any of your patients. Keep sending them to whoever you have been sending them to over the years."

He didn't know what to say, but I had the satisfaction of calling his bluff. As time went on, I earned the respect of all the doctors in the community and their patients. And my practice grew. Because there were no other surgeons in town that could assist me in surgery, I had to use the general practitioners in town as assistants. They helped me to operate on major cases that I did on their patients. They were very capable as assistants, and appreciative of the fact that they could be more closely involved in the total care of their patients.

One poor devil that I helped had a previous history of gonorrhea. He was a black male, who over the years had developed a stricture of the urethra (opening from the bladder through the penis). His scrotum was larger than a basketball, and his urine came out through several fistulous openings in this grossly enlarged scrotum instead of through his penis. It is known as a water-pot perineum because of the many leaky openings. All he could do was cover it with rags to catch most of the urine. He also had difficulty walking because of the size of his scrotum. He needed help badly. My friend asked me to help. I told him that first we had to divert the stream of urine by putting a tube in his bladder with a clamp on it. Then when he had to go, all he had to do was open the clamp and drain his bladder. Once the stream of urine was controlled, we could clear up any infection present. Because the stream of urine was diverted, the scrotum would shrink in size, and in three months I could resect most of the excess scrotum and reestablish the flow of urine normally through the penis. I saw him in the office a few times. His scrotum was not leaking, and it was decreasing in size. He was tickled to death with his new arrangement. Unfortunately, before he was ready for his definitive surgery, he disappeared. My friend and I assumed that he liked his bladder tube so well that he decided to keep it that way.

One of my requests from administration when I went to Crestview to operate was to purchase a few basic vascular instruments. They happily obliged. It was almost prophetic, and having them on hand at the time was critical in saving one man's life. A short time after the instruments arrived they were put to good use.

A young man arrived at the hospital emergency room in Crestview after being shot in a deer hunting accident in which he suffered a gunshot wound from buckshot. Someone mistook him for a deer. Buckshot from a shotgun contains large pellets that can do severe damage. This man had several pellets in his liver, wounds to his large and small bowel, and most critical were the through-and-through perforations of the inferior vena cava (largest vein in the body, with a diameter of over one inch). He was taken to surgery, where I was able to close the four perforations of the vena cava and stop the blood loss. I next closed the perforations in the large and small bowel, and sutured the lesions in the liver. His blood loss was replaced, and he recovered uneventfully. This was a very lucky young man, having a surgeon and a very competent nurse anesthetist available in this small twenty-five-bed hospital to save his life. The nearest surgeon and MD anesthesiologist were sixty miles away, and I doubt that at the rate he was bleeding that he would have been able to make that trip.

Cancer of the esophagus is a very serious disease, and the cure rate is not good at all. Dr. Ochsner told us as students about a surgeon in South America who had operated on many patients who had cancer of the esophagus with only one survivor. His comment was, "One candle is better than utter darkness." The results are better now, but it still is very serious surgery. One of my patients in Crestview had a cancer of the lower third of the esophagus and was unable to swallow solid food at all when I saw him. He had lost a lot of weight and asked me if I could do anything for him.

He had only two options: one was for me to place a feeding tube into his stomach, (gastrostomy) a fairly simple procedure, and the other was to go through a very complicated procedure with higher risk, and replace his esophagus with his colon so that he could eat.

In training in Mobile, we were dealing with a low socioeconomic group in which cancer of the esophagus is more common. I took care of many cases of this type of cancer, and several forms of treatment were used. We did gastrostomies, placing plastic tubes through the tumor (very temporary), removing the cancer and the esophagus, and replacing it by bringing the stomach into the chest. The stomach is then sewn to the upper esophagus as a replacement, and the patient is then able to eat normally.

My favorite procedure was to use the colon as a substitute for the esophagus. In this procedure, the esophagus is removed, and part of the colon is then brought into the chest with its own blood supply, sewn to the upper esophagus above, and to the stomach below. It is a major procedure, but it works very well. When I left my residency, I had performed many of these procedures, more than any other surgeon in Mobile had at that time.

My patient was told about his options, and I explained the risks and possible poor prognosis. He elected to have the major procedure done and said he would give anything to be able to eat again. I did the four-hour surgery, and he had an uneventful post-operative course. He ate everything in sight, and you've never seen a happier guy. Unfortunately, he died six months later of metastasis but he ate heartily until his death. I think going through the surgery was worth it to him.

These patients I just described were indigent patients, and I saw a lot of them, but I received a great deal of satisfaction by performing the service. Money was scarce in Crestview in 1960.

I opened my office in Fort Walton Beach Florida approximately three months after arriving in Okaloosa County. The first three months I was able to practice in Ceorge Barrow's office in Crestview and do surgery at their 25-bed hospital. Fort Walton Beach at this time also had a 25-bed hospital with two operating rooms and two nurse anesthetists. The staff was very capable, but I must admit I was quite apprehensive about opening a surgical practice in this small area with limited facilities. I came to town as the first surgeon in the county, and I was doctor number eleven. Most of the general practitioners had limited surgical privileges, and they were quite capable. Cases that were beyond the level of expertise of the GPs were being sent to Pensacola for their surgery (50 miles away). There was no local pathologist, and a pathology firm in Pensacola was used for this service. We were limited as to what we could do; for example there was no capability to do frozen sections when doing breast biopsies checking for cancer of the breast. Any biopsies that were done were sent to Pensacola for analysis, and we had to wait for results.

One amusing incident occurred on a day that I happened to be driving to Pensacola. One of the lab techs asked me to deliver a package (a specimen) to the pathologist's office while I was going there. I said, "Okay, what is it?"

He said, "It's a leg that had been amputated."

I said, "Okay, put it in the trunk, and I'll deliver it."

On my way there, I got to thinking, what if I were stopped by the highway patrol, how would I talk my way out of this? They probably would arrest me and claim I was a mass murderer! I was glad to get that parcel delivered.

When I arrived in town, I was determined to follow my specialty in surgery. I had received excellent training, and I didn't want to put my specialty aside and do general practice. Not that general practice is not important, but I could have done that without spending the time that I did specializing four years earlier. To do this, it soon became obvious that I would have to do some traveling. In Okaloosa County, there was a twenty-five-bed hospital in Crestview, a twenty-bed hospital in Valparaiso, and a twenty-five-bed hospital in Fort Walton Beach. There was also a twenty-five-bed hospital sixty miles north in the small Alabama town of Florala. None of these had a trained surgeon, so doctors from all of these areas called on me to do surgery in their respective communities. This I was able to do, and usually made rounds on these patients daily. The roads were empty, except for an occasional farm tractor, and I usually drove at speeds of up to 100 miles an hour. Highway patrolmen were scarce, so I was able to move on with no interference. This kept me busy, but it was the only way that I could keep up a surgical practice in this small area.

Living in the country has many advantages, and also some disadvantages. One interesting experience happened in my office one day while I was seeing patients. As I went from one exam room to the other, I saw a snake in the hallway. I thought that it was fake, and that my nurse was playing a trick on me. As I bent over to pick it up, the snake moved. It was alive, and it was a pigmy rattler. Apparently it had come through the side door, and no one had seen it. I then tried to capture it and put it outside. It's a fun experience to try to get a live snake into a round waste basket, but patience prevailed, and I was able to accomplish the task and then put the snake back out in the bushes where he belonged. This wouldn't happen in a city practice.

Another incident involving a pigmy rattler was when I was out playing golf. Walking out of a hazard, I came to the steps leading out. Behind the steps was a growth of weeds and foliage. As I started up the steps, I felt a severe stinging sensation. It felt like a bee sting, and I thought that I had been stung by a hornet. After I got up the steps, my leg reddened and began to swell. Within minutes, my leg had turned red, and I had marked swelling and acute pain. I was quite a distance from the clubhouse, so naturally I continued to play (ha, ha). After about 30 minutes, the pain subsided, and the swelling decreased. I then went to see my friend, Dr. Russell and told him the story. After he examined my leg, he found a wound that had broken the skin. Instead of a puncture wound that you would expect from a bee sting, he found a tangential wound. He had seen and treated many snake bites, and he told me that a pigmy rattler had bitten me. He said that they have poor vision, and he hit me with a glancing blow. By then, my leg was recovering, and I needed no further treatment. I'm glad it wasn't a direct hit.

On occasion, in the emergency room, we would see a patient who had been bitten by a snake. Some were quite serious and had to be treated with anti venom. They usually survived, but some of them were quite ill until they recovered.

Another interesting country experience was when a patient came into the emergency room after having been bitten by an alligator. It was a hot summer day, and this man happened to be driving by a small lake. The water looked inviting, so he decided to go for a swim. While in the lake, he was attacked by an alligator. The alligator tore his arm off, and he was lucky to escape. When he arrived at the emergency room, his stump was repaired, and he lived to tell about it, but he lost an arm.

I drove about 40,000 miles a year during that time. Dr. Maxon, who had asked me previously if I was a pro when I first came to town, used to tease me about my travel. He called me "Palladin." I said "What do you mean by that?"

He said, "You know, have knife, will travel," comparing me to TV's Palladin in, *Have Gun, Will Travel.*

Chapter Twelve
Florala

The town of Florala brings back many good memories. They had a twenty-five-bed hospital and two general practitioners but no surgeon. A very fine gentleman whose name is Seymour Gittenstein owned a shirt factory there, and in his generosity, he had the hospital built for the town. He was very proud of it and wanted the town to have good medical care, which he subsidized. He approached me to see if I would do surgery at the Florala Hospital. I wasn't too sure about this, since the hospital was sixty miles away from my office in Fort Walton Beach, but I thought I would try it. Traveling back and forth to check on my patients was time consuming, but the patients were so happy to be able to have their surgery near home, and they were so grateful, that it made it worthwhile. They also gave me the red-carpet treatment when I came to town. People in this area were not wealthy, and my collection percentage was only about fifty percent, but I felt that I was providing a service to some very fine people. I loved them, and it was worth it. Sometimes I was paid in fruits and vegetables by grateful patients.

There was an older population in Florala, and I did quite a number of hip nailings. Many of these patients were not able to travel to another hospital, and could not afford the care. I did a lot of the surgery gratis, and the hospital absorbed the cost. We had a pathetic little 50-ma x-ray machine, so it was not possible to follow the surgery by x-ray; it only worked if the patient weighed eighty pounds. It was a joke.

Fortunately, I had been trained to open the capsule around the hip joint and align the fracture before driving a nail over the fracture site. This was done by feel and experience, and it worked. After a couple of years, I invested in a single-engine airplane and began to fly back and forth. I had to use a very short crop duster's strip that was grassed, but one third of it was full of ruts, and that part of the runway was really unuseable. It had high tension wires at the north end, so I had to approach the strip from the south, and also depart to the south. It was slightly wider than the wings on the airplane. My earlier training as a carrier pilot making short field landings came in handy. I would buzz the hospital, and when they heard me, they would come to the strip, which was about six miles away, to pick me up. In the afternoon after work, they would take me back to the airplane, and I would fly home. It was great fun.

One day, a Navy flight surgeon from nearby Pensacola evidently not too experienced in flying, flew to Florala to work in their emergency room. He was a member of the Navy's Aero Club, and he knew that I had been flying in and out of the small strip that I called the Paxton International Airport, so he thought he would try it. He came in over the high tension wires, landed with too much speed, went through the south fence, and ended up in the trees. He was unhurt, but the airplane was a mess and had to be taken back to Pensacola in pieces.

Another experience that I will not forget was a day when I had to have maintenance done on the airplane, so I flew the airplane to Birmingham to pick up a pilot, who would then take the airplane back to Birmingham for maintenance. When the work was completed, he would fly it back to me at the Paxton International Airport, and I would fly him home. This was a good plan until he came back and was approaching the field with the landing gear not extended. I watched in horror and could see him landing gear up and destroying my airplane.

Fortunately, a friend of mine who used that strip as a crop duster saw what was happening, and had the presence of mind to jump out on the landing strip and waved him off. He then realized what he had done, and went around, this time putting the gear down, and landed, a very embarrassed pilot. My friend was given a bottle of Crown Royal as a token of my appreciation for saving my airplane.

As time went on, cases that needed closer observation or more specialized surgery, I transferred to Fort Walton Beach where I could be closer to the patient and give better supervision. One of these cases transferred to me from Florala was a teen-aged girl who had been in an auto accident. Her physician in Florala was quite astute in diagnosing the presence of an acute abdomen in this patient. She was transferred to Fort Walton Beach and evaluated. She did indeed have an acute (tender and painful) abdomen, and evidence of blood loss. In those days, there were no special techniques for easy diagnosis. MRI and CT scans had not been invented. All we could do to try to determine the presence or absence of blood in the abdomen was to insert a needle into the abdomen and try to extract blood. This was a primitive approach, but it is all that we had other than watch her hemoglobin drop. In this case her acute abdomen was the result of a ruptured spleen sustained in an auto accident. On exploration, I found a badly damaged spleen with active bleeding ,and I performed a splenectomy, which then stopped the bleeding. She recovered without any complications, and I had a very grateful patient, family, and referring physician. This was the first of many patient referrals that I was later to receive from Florala.

Another interesting case from that area comes to mind. This was a seventy-five-year-old, white female who had shortness of breath and chest discomfort. She had been seen in the tumor clinic in Pensacola by a group of doctors from different specialties that see interesting patients and also charity cases. After evaluation, she was told that she had cancer of the lung, and that nothing could be done for her.

I reviewed her records and chest x-rays, and she had a mass in the center of her chest (mediastium), that was displacing other structures in that area. Her x-rays had not changed in over a year, and I just couldn't buy the diagnosis given to her that she had inoperable cancer. I discussed the possibilities with her, and since she was in good health,

I transferred her to Fort Walton Beach, and we elected to operate. I opened her chest, and removed the mediastinal mass intact. The pathologist diagnosed it as a benign mediastinal tumor. She was cured and went home a very happy patient.

Some weeks later, word had gotten back to the Pensacola tumor clinic about the surgery, and the happy result. One of the doctors called me to congratulate me on the success of this operation and was embarrassed that they had missed this diagnosis.

I did quite a bit of surgery in Florala, including appendectomies, hernia repairs, hysterectomies, both abdominal and vaginal, tonsillectomies and other procedures. The larger, more complicated cases I took to Fort Walton Beach where the facilities were more modern and I could follow the patients more closely. I reluctantly ended this episode in my life when I got so busy that I was not able to give quality care to patients that far out of town and still take care of my practice in Fort Walton Beach. I still saw patients from Florala, but my days of doing surgery at the Florala hospital came to a close.

On occasion, I had to go to Milton, Florida, to do surgery. A doctor friend of mine practiced in that area in the small town of Pace. He and I were friends when I was a resident in Mobile and he was an intern. He married a nurse who was at the Mobile General Hospital at the time, and we were all friends. He practiced in Pace and did all of his hospital work at the Milton hospital.

One day he called me and told me that his wife had developed cancer of the breast, and asked me if I would come to Milton to do a mastectomy. I readily agreed, and did a mastectomy on her at the Milton Hospital. I drove back and forth to see her daily until she was discharged. She did quite well. Many years have passed, and when I last heard, she was doing well and had no signs of recurrence. It was a happy experience.

Chapter Thirteen
Early Cases

Getting started in practice was very difficult, especially when you start with a family (wife and two kids) and no money. I had what you would call a negative financial statement. If I sold everything I had, I would still have debt. During my first three months in town I had to borrow money to survive. I had no collateral. All that I had was the fact that I had completed thirteen years of training, had an MD degree, and the determination to finish in spite of the fact that I had a family.

Armed with that, I went to my local banker, Lewie Tidwell, who had only been with the bank one week, and asked him for a five-hundred-dollar loan. Because he had only been there one week, he said that he had to go to the president, Mr. Taylor, for approval. I returned in two days and was told that Mr. Taylor would not approve the loan. I was in disbelief! Didn't the fact that I had an MD degree qualify me for a measly five-hundred-dollar loan? Apparently not.

The struggle and poverty continued until I could start receiving some fees for services. I later went to another bank for a $2500 loan. This new bank approved the loan only if I had three cosigners on the note. I asked three friends to cosign with me, and they did. These were true friends, and I'm grateful to them to this day. One was a restaurant owner, another a car dealer, and the third was a fellow MD. Dr. Geisen, Pete Testa, and Warren Taylor were my benefactors.

Finally my practice began to grow, and I was able to pay off my debt and take care of my family. I was able to rent an office space across the street from the hospital. It was in a house that I converted to an office, and I practiced there for a year before I entered a clinic that was well established in the area.

I started at one thousand a month the first year, and then went to fifteen hundred a month in my second year. I also had to contribute ten thousand dollars to the clinic to join. The third year, I went on a percentage, and my income dropped to five hundred dollars a month. I thought that by joining the clinic that my income would increase; instead I was going backwards. The problem was that they sold me on getting into the clinic as the only surgeon, but two other members of the group were also doing general surgery cases as part of their practice. There wasn't enough surgery to go around.

I gave them an ultimatum: "Refer surgery to me that you brought me into the clinic to do, or I will leave. I cannot live on five hundred a month. " Besides this, I was driving all over the county doing surgery at other hospitals at my own expense. They refused, so I left and spent the rest of my practice years essentially solo. I left the initial deposit of ten thousand dollars with the clinic as part of the deal. It was either that or be prohibited from practicing in this area for a period of two years. That was not an acceptable option, so I remained in town, and it was worth the gamble in the long run.

I wasn't the only poor professional in town. One day in my early years, I saw a new lawyer in town in my office who had just finished law school and was just as poor as I was. He had an emergency with one of his children, and he came to me for help. This child had aspirated a "jack"while playing. This many-pronged object became lodged in her vocal cords, and she was having respiratory distress.

He was very concerned and asked if I could take care of the problem. I said I could and would, so I had the patient put to sleep, and with a laryngoscope was able to see the metal jack and remove it. It was a simple but very effective procedure. I then presented the parents with the cause of her breathing problem, the jack. She came out to a pair of very grateful parents. His question to me then was, "How much do I owe you?"

I said, "You owe me one scotch and soda, payable at some time in the future."

He said, "You're kidding!"

I said, "No, I'm not; that's all that you owe me."

He was forever grateful, and I was very pleased to be able to help him in his time of need. He later paid off his debt, we were both happy, and we became lifetime friends.

In those days, there were very few anesthesiologists in the state of Florida, and none in our area. Anesthesia had to be given by nurse anesthetists, who did very well, but they had their limitations. The first open chest case that was done in Okaloosa County was a case that I performed in the twenty-five-bed hospital in Fort Walton Beach. The patient was a young, black male who came to the emergency room with a stab wound of the chest. The doctor on call, Dr. Russell, examined him, and found that he was in shock but still alive. He started some blood on him, and called for me. Examination revealed the stab wound and no breath sounds in his right chest, and we prepared him for surgery.

We wasted no time, but we had one problem; the anesthetists had never given anesthesia for an open-chest case. We had no choice but to open his chest, which was full of blood, and stop the bleeding. I told them that I would talk the anesthetists through it. First I intubated the patient so that we would have positive control of his breathing. Then we put him to sleep and opened his chest. I had to coach the anesthetist on how hard and how often to expand the now exposed lung.

When the chest is open, unless the patient is intubated and respiration controlled, the lung collapses. All of this is controlled by feel. I was then able to remove the blood from the chest cavity and find the source of bleeding. The bleeding was coming from the internal mammary artery that had been completely severed, and I stopped the bleeding by ligating the vessel.

By then, he had received enough blood that his blood pressure started to return to normal. The chest was then closed, chest tubes were inserted for drainage, and he was sent to the recovery room. The patient recovered without complications. It was an easy and gratifying case, but it made history as the first chest operation ever performed in the county. More important, we saved his life.

EUGENE R. CELANO, M.D.

A case that I remember very well was in the early days at the Fort Walton Beach Hospital. Dr. Russell and I were doing a hernia repair on his nurses son, (a young boy two or three years of age) during the procedure, he developed laryngospasm (vocal cords closed and would not allow air to pass through). Needless to say, this situation created some panic with the nurse anesthetist who was giving anesthesia. She let us know as the child was turning blue.

I immediately broke scrub, and inserted an endotracheal tube so that the anesthetist could then breath for the patient. This corrected the problem, and we went ahead with the surgery, and the child was fine. It turned out some years later that the mother of that child came to work for me as an office nurse for many years. She was and still is an excellent nurse and a wonderful person.

One day while doing a tonsillectomy on a child, the child's mother tried to force her way into the operating room. We knew that she was a little nutty, but I did not expect this kind of behavior. She was stopped, but became very hostile afterward.

That afternoon at my office, she came in at closing time, and I told my office nurse not to leave. I was concerned about the mental stability of this lady. As I came out of my office to see her, she reached into her purse, and I thought, *Here it is, I'm going to get it.* I moved closer to her. Thinking that she was going to pull a gun on me, I wanted to be close enough to her so that I could grab it. It turned out that she did not have a gun, but it somewhat unnerved me at the time. A week or so later, she called me at home in the middle of the night with some irrational story that the governor of Mississippi was going to come after me (reason unknown). The woman was mentally ill.

It's somewhat usual for a surgeon to operate on his family. In a large city many surgeons are available to operate on other doctor's family, but in a small town, that is not the case. You have the choice of taking them to another city to an unknown physician or do the work yourself. I chose to do surgery on my family on two separate occasions. One time I did a bilateral inguinal hernia repair on my son when he was five years old. On another occasion, I operated on my mother when she had gall stones and gallbladder disease. I couldn't think of anyone that would do these surgeries with more at stake and with more care than I would.

They both did well, and I was happy with the end result. They say that it is too emotional for one to operate on his own family, but I was able to divorce myself of the emotions and concentrate on the job that had to be done.

An attorney friend of mine went to Mexico to go scuba diving, and while on this trip sustained an injury to his hand. He had a spear gun to use in case of an encounter with a shark. This spear gun had a shotgun shell in it so that if it was struck forcefully against a shark the shell would go off and the spear would then penetrate the shark or fish.

Not having encountered any sharks on this trip, he decided that he would see if it would work. He jammed the spear into a rock with his hand at the other end, and it worked, but the end that was in his hand backfired and went completely through his hand. He then wrapped his hand in a towel, packed his bags, and flew home.

The next day this is how I saw him. He didn't trust the Mexican doctors, so he thought that he would save this gift for me. It was a mess, and all that I could do at the time was to clean it up, put him on antibiotics, and then later repair it. He was fortunate in that he ended up with no bone or nerve injury and a good useable hand.

Doctors strive for perfection and good results on their patients, especially where risks are ever present. Unfortunately, this is not always the case, and one of these sad memories I have to live with involved a newborn child less than two weeks old. The child had duodenal atresia. Earlier I mentioned the paper that I had presented to a meeting of the Alabama Chapter of the American College of Surgeons about a 16-day-old child with duodenal atresia with survival. This problem at birth is a rare occurrence, so I was delighted to again have the opportunity to perform this operation.

We brought in an M.D. anesthesiologist from a nearby city to give anesthesia, because I felt that the case was too delicate for our nurse anesthetists to handle.

This baby was hydrated and well prepared for surgery. The abdomen was opened, and the obstruction located. I brought the jejunum (small bowel) up to the duodenum to bypass the obstruction and sutured it in place.

Frequent checks with the anesthesiologist told me that anesthesia was going well. Blood loss was minimal, and the surgery took less than an hour. As I started to close the abdomen, the anesthesiologist told me that the baby was dead.

I was totally shocked. "What do you mean, he's dead? How can that be?" The surgery had gone too well.

This was not a surgical death; this was an anesthetic death. He was evidently oversedated and given too much anesthesia. Try to explain that to the parents! How can you forget it when the surgery went smoothly without a problem, and then you're told that the baby died an anesthetic death? This was truly a sad experience for all involved.

Then there are good experiences, when you know that if you had not been in the community that a patient with a severe injury would not have been able to make the trip to a hospital where a surgeon could help him. Such a case happened in the early 1960s, shortly after my arrival in town. A hurricane was brewing, and my wife and I and another couple were returning home from an evening out. We decided to go look at the waves and the rising waters at the local yacht club as the storm was approaching. After that, we headed for home, and on the way, we arrived at the scene of an accident. An auto had hit the concrete abutment at the entry to the Cinco Bayou Bridge head on. The accident had happened only minutes before we arrived on the scene.

The driver and the front seat passenger were slumped over and in obvious distress. An ambulance was called, and while we waited, we pulled the driver and the front seat passenger out of the car. The driver was not too badly hurt, but the passenger was semi-conscious and in shock, probably from internal bleeding. No one was wearing a seat belt. The passenger had hit the dashboard with his right side and sustained internal and facial injuries. By then the ambulance had arrived, and we helped load the injured into the ambulance. We followed the ambulance to the hospital, and in the emergency room, the blood pressure had dropped out of sight and was unattainable. I knew that if we didn't get some blood in him soon, and then stop his bleeding, that he would die. Because of the critical situation, we started a couple of bottles of O-negative blood (no crossmatch) and prepared the operating room for exploratory surgery. His blood pressure started back up as he received the blood, and I was ready to get into his abdomen and stop the bleeding.

My friend, a local GP, was concerned about his facial lacerations, and was working on them, and I told him to forget these for now; if we don't get his bleeding stopped he wouldn't have to worry about his facial scars. Wasting no time, the patient was put to sleep, his abdomen prepped, and opened. When I got in there, his abdomen was full of blood that had to be removed to find the source of bleeding. The bleeding was coming from multiple fractures of the liver. It looked like a ripe watermelon that had been dropped and split open. It had several deep tears in it. I could put my hand deep into the liver.

I controlled the bleeding and was able to place multiple sutures in the liver to reconstruct the organ. The liver is difficult to suture; thin sutures tear through the substance of the liver and its capsule, so large-caliber cat gut sutures were carefully put in place. Because the fractured liver leaks bile as well as blood, there is always the danger of bile peritonitis, which can also be fatal. The omentum, which is called the guardian of the abdomen, was wrapped over his injured liver. This is a fatty layer that often migrates to any injury or infection in the abdomen and helps to protect and keep the injured area localized.

After that, multiple rubber drains were put in place so that any bile or blood drainage would be directed outside of the abdomen. With the bleeding stopped, his blood pressure began to rise to normal levels, and his abdomen was closed. Considering the type of injury he had, he recuperated very well. His hospital stay was only ten days, and he was released to be followed as an outpatient.

Three months after his surgery, he was back to skydiving and jumping out of airplanes. This was a very good result and a very gratifying experience for both of us.

On occasion, I would be called upon to go the Eglin Air Force base hospital to do surgery. They had a medical staff available at that facility, but occasionally they ran into cases that were beyond the capability of the surgeon on their staff, and I was called upon to help out in these emergencies, cases such as gunshot wounds, chest cases, or major abdominal cases.

One unusual and interesting case was that of a male patient that had developed bleeding from his stomach. What was interesting was that this patient had been in good health until this bleeding began. He had taken one and only one adult aspirin prior to the development of the bleeding episode. In spite of all of the efforts by the medical team, and after his receiving four units of blood, they were unable to slow the loss of blood.

At that point I was called in to consult, and finally decided that the only way to stop the bleeding was through surgical intervention. I performed a gastrectomy and removed most of his stomach, and that stopped all bleeding. What was so unusual was that only one aspirin could cause all of that bleeding.

I love animals, and have had numerous dogs as pets in the past. While in Mobile, I had a Boston Terrier that I really loved, and he would recognize my car as I came home from work. One night when I came home late, it was dark, and I turned into the driveway at my home. I didn't see him, nor realize that he had run out and ran under the back wheels of the car. I was devastated. I took him to the vet, and he found a fractured pelvis and a broken leg, but no internal injuries. He put a pin in his leg and wrapped him in tape, and I took him home to take care of him. He recovered from his injury, and had the pin removed from his leg after he had healed.

About a year and a half later, after moving to Fort Walton Beach, my dog began to have frequent diarrhea. (This sometimes happens when the colon is obstructed.) The stool breaks down, liquefies, and tries to go around the obstruction.

I took the dog to the only veterinarian in town. (This was a small town.) He diagnosed the obstruction in the colon by passing a glass rod up into the rectum until it hit a very hard object; a collection of bones that had blocked the bowel, and would only allow passage of fluid around the obstruction. He then told me that the dog was obstructed, but that he could not do that kind of surgery. I said, "Well, by golly I can and will before I'll let my pet die."

With that, I took my puppy down to the clinic emergency room, showed my friend, Dr. Thompson, (a pediatrician) how to administer ether for anesthesia, and we put the dog to sleep. I opened the abdomen and found the obstruction, which was composed of two masses of chicken bones about two inches in diameter each. I opened the colon, removed the masses, closed the colon and the abdomen, wrapped his little body with tape, and woke him up. He was unsteady for a day or two but recovered rapidly, as dogs do, and went on to live out a full life.

When the vet found out what I had done, he kiddingly told me that he was going to start operating on humans. I said "Go ahead, be my guest." I took a lot of kidding after that, but I saved my sweet little puppy dog.

Chapter Fourteen
Chest Surgery

Surgery of the chest was and still is considered very major surgery, and it was my favorite type of surgery. It is interesting, intricate, exhausting at times, but very satisfying to both the patient and the surgeon. I was fortunate during my training to have the opportunity to perform many chest cases under excellent supervision. The best part of all of this was that they supervised and taught, and never took over the case. This is the best way for a student to learn.

There were several surgeons on the teaching staff in Mobile very capable of handling surgery of the chest, but two that stand out in my memory are Curtis Smith and Earnest Debakey. They were both excellent technicians, and they made hard cases look easy by making each move a step in the procedure. Lungs diseased by tuberculosis are very difficult to operate on because of extent of the disease and the scarring that makes it difficult to separate the structures. We operated on a number of these cases at the sixth district tuberculosis hospital in Mobile, Alabama.

I did many pneumonectomies, lobectomies, esophageal resections, and treated gunshot wounds of the chest. I could put in chest tubes for drainage in my sleep. I will describe some of the cases that I had involving chest trauma and malignancies. This type of surgery requires extra care and skill to accomplish some of the procedures done in the chest, including partial or complete removal of a lung, or esophageal surgery. I never did open-heart surgery (except in a few gunshot wounds). This type of surgery was developed after my training and became a field of its own, with extensive sophisticated equipment. Heart/lung machines came into being that were used when the heart was stopped to work on it, and the machine took over the function of pumping blood and breathing.

There are special problems in surgery of the chest that do not apply in other types of surgery. For example, the incision for opening the chest is much longer. This is so that the relatively rigid ribs can be spread without breaking them. Usually to make enough room to work you need to either remove a rib, or a part of it. You then use a rib spreader to open the wound so that you have enough room to work. Dissection of blood vessels and lung tissue is more delicate than most other tissue and requires more care. You are dealing with large vessels in a small area, which are sometimes friable and easy to tear. Also in lung resections, care must be taken to seal off the bronchus so that no air leaks will develop after surgery.

The most common procedure in chest surgery is removal of part of the lung, (lobectomy) or pneumonectomy (all of the lung on one side of the chest cavity). This leaves a space that fills with blood or expansion of the remaining lung.

After closing the chest, tubes are inserted into the chest cavity. These are necessary to help expand the lung. These tubes lead to sealed, under-water traps so that when the patient breathes, the lung gradually expands, and leaks in the lung, if present, gradually seal. After the lung expands, and the leaks stop, the chest tubes are removed. The space where the lung had been removed fills with fluid, and also there is a shift and expansion of the remaining lung into that area.

Aftercare of post-op surgical patients is very important, especially after chest surgery. It is important to clear out secretions to prevent pneumonia and to be constantly aware of the possibility of infection or leaks in the lung or bronchus. If all went well after this surgery, I would plan on six weeks for full recovery. These examples of surgery are fairly routine, but the surgeon has to be prepared for many different situations. This is where judgement and experience pay off.

A gentleman referred to me from Defuniak Springs, Florida, came to see me with his x-rays that showed a malignant lesion in his right lung. He needed surgery. In these cases, where the lesion is determines how much of the lung has to be taken out to result in hope for a cure. In this case, the lesion was close to the hilum (area where the bronchial tubes and the blood vessels originate in the chest). It was possible that he would have to have the entire right lung removed. Pulmonary function studies were done, and it was determined that he would be able to withstand a pneumonectomy.

I did the surgery, and the patient did well. Follow up showed no return of the malignancy for five years. Sometime later, a follow up - ray showed that he had developed a small lesion on his left lung. Now what? Could he tolerate more surgery? Could he afford to lose more lung? I decided to do a wedge resection, because I felt that he would not be able to tolerate taking out any more lung. Surprisingly, he tolerated this quite well and was sent home to be followed as an outpatient.

It turned out that this was an entirely different cell type than the tumor that had previously been removed from the right side where he had undergone pneumonectomy over five years before. The two lesions were not at all related.

I followed him as an outpatient for two more years, during which time he was doing well, then I lost track of him. I suspect that he probably died from the second lesion, because I could take no more lung than I did, and what I took was probably not enough to cure him.

Smoking is a horrible habit. I can't say enough negative things about it. Its effect on the lungs and cardiovascular system are devastating. Another patient that I took care of had what is called severe bullous emphysema. This is where portions of the lung, because of to extreme emphysema, expand into small and large balloon-like structures that take up valuable space, compressing good lung. This prevents the normal exchange of oxygen by the lungs. The patient in severe cases becomes very short of breath, even at rest. The treatment is to open the chest, resect these blebs, and free up good lung, which enables the patient to breathe easier. In selected cases, this is a very helpful piece of surgery.

A condition that occasionally requires opening the chest is a condition called spontaneous pneumothorax. Essentially the lung collapses for no apparent reason. This frequently happens in young patients, but can happen at any age. The individual usually experiences chest pain and sometimes shortness of breath, depending on how much of the lung collapses. The treatment is insertion of a chest tube attached to underwater drainage. As the lung expands, the air bubbles out into a bottle containing water, and the weight of the water prevents the air from going back into the chest. If there is a large leak, it may bubble constantly until it closes the leak by coming in contact with the chest wall. On occasion, the chest has to be opened, the leak found, and closed. At the same time, the chest inner wall is roughened so that when the lung expands, it will stick to the chest wall and not collapse again.

One day, I operated on a male who had cancer of the lung from smoking. The lung is divided into two lobes on the left, and three lobes on the right. In surgery for cancer of the lung, you may have to take out a lobe (lobectomy), or the whole lung (pneumonectomy), depending on the location and accessability of the lesion. In this case I was able to do a lobectomy. Up until this time, I had been a smoker, and after the surgery, I went to the dining room to have a cup of coffee and a cigarette. After I lit up, I said to my assistant, "Why am I doing this? Am I crazy?" with that, I put out the cigarette and never smoked again. I knew better, but looking at the cancer I had just removed and the black lung the patient had finally convinced me. From that time on, my classmate, Dr. Russell, and I carried on a crusade about the hazards of smoking. We convinced a number of patients to stop smoking.

In those days, there were no other surgeons available to assist me in the various operations in which it was necessary to have an assistant surgeon. I used several different general practitioners to help. The protocol was that if you were referred a case, it was expected that you would ask the referring doctor to assist you in operating on his patient. This was the case one day when I had scheduled the patient of a doctor friend of mine for surgery. This patient had clinical and x-ray findings of cancer of the lung, and thoracotomy was indicated. We did not know until the chest was opened whether or not we could do a lobectomy or a pneumonectomy. It turned out that I was able to do a lobectomy, and while dissecting out the vessels and the bronchus, I noticed that my assistant had a slight cough. He had a mask on, but it became obvious that something unusual was going on.

I said, "How long have you had this cough?"

He said, "Oh, it's only a cigarette cough. (He had been a smoker for many years.)

I said, "Okay, but when I finish this case, I'm going to take you to the x-ray department and get a chest x-ray on you."

He reluctantly agreed, and I took him over to the x-ray department and had the technician take a chest x-ray. When I saw the film, I saw a four-five-cm. lesion in his right lung. I knew then that he had a cancer of the lung. With that information and some additional studies, we prepared him for surgery about a week later.

The surgery consisted of a lobectomy and a lymph node dissection, which showed that some of the nodes were positive for cancer. He had further treatment, but to no avail. His health gradually declined over the next few months, and he died from his cancer of the lung. It was quite upsetting finding a cancer on a friend, operating on him, and then losing him because of metastasis of the tumor. The cure rate for cancer of the lung is not good, but I often wonder if I could have saved him if this lesion had been found sooner.

Over the years I have operated on many patients for cancer of the lung, and many of them were cured. The best way to cure cancer of the lung is to prevent its occurrence by never smoking in the first place. The next best bet, if you are a smoker is to quit. I can't in a few words explain or point out the dangers of smoking. When I grew up, everyone smoked, and we didn't think of its dangers. Now, there is no doubt about how dangerous a habit it really is. There are a small percentage of patients who develop cancer of the lung that are not cigarette smokers, but these are in the minority.

Surgery is not always performed without complications. Decisions have to be made during a procedure, because things are not always the way you see it in the textbooks. One such case that comes to mind was a case in which I was doing a lobectomy for chronic pulmonary disease of the right lung (bronchiectasis). I had as an assistant a surgeon who also practiced in the Fort Walton Beach area. He was well trained and qualified, but had a pretty good impression of himself, and it was difficult for him to play the role of an assistant. He sometimes became too aggressive and interfered with the surgeon in charge of the operation, me. This is very annoying and distracting to the surgeon who is responsible for the case.

This case was especially delicate because I was dealing with inflammatory reaction from the chronic lung disease, and I knew exactly what I was doing, but being cautious. While I was carefully dissecting out the vessels at the hilum of the lung, a small amount of bleeding developed in this area. My assistant took it upon himself to stop this small bleeder by putting a large metal clamp blindly into this area before I could stop him. By doing so, he cut halfway through the pulmonary artery. All hell broke loose, and blood welled up in the chest cavity. Needless to say I was really "pissed," and he was quite embarrassed to have done something so stupid. I controlled the bleeding and then carefully sutured the laceration in the pulmonary artery. I could then go on with the lobectomy and complete the procedure. The patient recovered nicely, and never knew how close she came to being a surgical death. Needless to say, I never used this doctor as an assistant ever again on any of my cases. It is very important to have an assistant that helps the surgeon instead of creating problems.

Over the years, surgery of the lung has changed very little. Attention to detail and close post-operative care is as important as it ever was. Many new procedures have been added to the surgeon's armamentarium with the advent of open-heart surgery and the ability to use the heart/lung machine. Arterial bypasses, use of stents, heart valve replacement, aortic grafts, atrial septal defects, removal of aneurysms, and even heart transplants can now be routinely accomplished. The practice of medicine has made amazing strides in the care of patients that were at one time untreatable.

Chapter Fifteen
All in a Day's Work

In general, I would like to describe a day in the life of a surgeon. It starts at six a.m. with a light breakfast, followed by a drive to the hospital to see patients that I had operated on earlier that week. I usually needed to see them not only to check their condition, but also to change orders if needed, change dressings, increase their diet, and tend to any of their needs before getting tied up in surgery for the day. Surgery usually started at seven-thirty a.m. and usually lasted until noon. Some days it was an all-day affair, depending on whether it was one case or several cases. If it was a long day, we would take a break between cases to rest, have a cup of coffee, go to the rest room, take care of emergencies, see consultations, or whatever. The operating rooms had to be cleaned between cases and prepared for the next patient, and this gave us time to take care of other problems.

In a small town with only one surgeon available, the surgical procedures were varied. It involved procedures from several specialties. In my practice I had to take care of cases involving orthopedics, ear nose and throat, gynecology, general surgery, thoracic surgery, vascular surgery, urology, and on rare occasions, obstetrics. In other words, I had to take care of whatever problem came along. On any one day, I would take out tonsils, fix a broken bones, fix a hernia, operate on a lung for cancer, remove a blood clot from an artery that was causing blockage to the leg, and occasionally do a cesarean section to deliver a baby.

The cases varied from day to day, and on some days when the schedule was light, we took that opportunity to catch up on our charts and records. This is paperwork all doctors hate to do. This time also gave me the opportunity to see other doctors' patients in consultation to see if they needed surgery or not. After a busy morning at the hospital, holding office hours in the afternoon was a necessity. In the office post-op patients were seen, as well as new patients, walk-ins, and referrals from other physicians. We also had to make arrangements with the hospital for scheduling surgery, arrange for a surgical assistant, and answer phone calls from patients, the hospital, and other physicians. There was always enough activity to keep me busy.

Every patient felt that his problem was the only problem in town, and rightly so. Because of a patient's concern, it took time to explain to them what had to be done in each case and reassure them of the outcome. Some patients who were very anxious took more time than others, but in all fairness, if I were in their shoes I would want the same treatment. After all, their surgery may be a once in a lifetime experience and should not be taken lightly.

After office hours I usually went back to the hospital to make evening rounds, and see all of my patients, especially those that had been operated on that day. I also had to see patients in consultation for future surgery. On occasion, I would be called to the emergency room to see a patient that needed surgery that evening. So much for going home!

After surgery, it was off to the house for supper and much-needed rest. Frequently I was called at night for various reasons. A patient problem, problems with orders left at the hospital, a sudden change in the condition of a post-op patient's status, and any number of other emergencies that might show up.

It's bad to be called out in the middle of the night for an emergency and while rushing to the hospital some jerk tries to race you and cut you off. This really tries your patience. One night while on the way to the hospital for an emergency, this very thing happened. I was speeding, and I tried to ignore this idiot without success. He continued to harass me until I got to the hospital. By then, my Italian temper took over, I parked the car, got out and said, "Okay, here I am! If you want me, come get me!"

With that, he turned his car around and left.

Another time while on the way to the emergency room, again speeding, one of the new local young policemen followed me and tried to stop me. First he put on his flashing lights, and I just kept going. Then, getting no response, he started blowing his horn. Still no response. Then he turned on his siren, and I kept right on going. When I arrived at the emergency room, he was furious, stopped his car and came toward me as I approached the hospital door. "Who the hell do you think you are?" I chuckled and said very calmly as I continued to walk away, "I'm Dr. Celano; that's who." I left him with a puzzled look on his face as he said, "How am I supposed to know?" and I went into the hospital smiling to take care of my emergency.

One advantage of being in a small town is that the police, sheriff's department, and highway patrol usually knew all the doctors and were always willing to do anything to help them. We would work well together when they brought accident victims to the hospital, so that we always had a good relationship with them.

One night, again speeding, a sheriff's car took off after me. It was a friend, Joe Johnson, and when he saw who it was, he got out in front of me, lights flashing and siren going, and gave me an escort to the hospital. They were very helpful to the medical staff.

One night when I was not on call, I was attending one of our big-time local events, the "Billy Bowlegs Ball." This was an event in which the locals celebrated the legendary pirate William Bowles, who was said to have his headquarters in our general area. It was similar to a Mardi Gras celebration, and each year a new Billy Bowlegs, along with his queen and honor guard, were elected to run the motley crew.

While partying that night, I was called to the phone. It was a local attorney. He had sustained a severe laceration of his hand and wanted me to come to the emergency room and repair his injured hand. His name was Dick Timmel, and I said, "Dick, I'm at this party, and I've had a couple of drinks. You need to get whoever is on call to sew you up."

He said, "I'd rather have you sew me up drunk than any of these other guys sober."

Although I had a couple of drinks, I wasn't drunk. I said, "Okay," and the sheriff drove me to the emergency room where I sewed up his lacerations. The sheriff then drove me back to the party.

I cannot imagine this happening today with a lawyer. I probably would have been sued. As it was, he got a good result and was quite appreciative.

I had as a patient a 9-year-old boy who had sustained a chest injury while staying at a local motel. He ran through a large plate glass window, and a heavy piece of the glass cut through his rib cage and went into his chest. This collapsed his lung, and when I saw him he was in distress, short of breath due to blood loss and the collapsed lung. The lung was contused and bleeding, but not seriously injured. At surgery, he was transfused, the bleeding was stopped, the chest wound was closed, and chest tubes were inserted. He recovered nicely and was sent home to Birmingham to be followed by his family physician after the chest tubes had been removed.

This was a relatively simple case, but I had some very grateful parents when it was all over.

As an addendum to this story, I chuckle as I recall my encounter with their attorney. He was an overbearing bully who had been in town a long time, and felt his importance by pushing the new doctor around. I received an unacceptable, insulting letter from him demanding a medical report of the accident and the surgery. When I received the letter, I asked a doctor friend of his, "Who the hell does he think he is?"

He said, "Oh, that's just Joe, and that's the way he is."

Then I threw the letter into the trash. About two weeks later, I was out at a local bar and restaurant and ran into this lawyer. He very abruptly asked me, "When the hell are you going to respond to my letter?"

I told him that I had thrown the letter in the trash, and that when he sent me a decent, professional letter, then I would respond to it. With that, I walked away.

I never saw an attorney speechless, but in this case he was. About a week later, he wrote me a very professional letter, and I then responded and gave him the information he requested. After that, we knew where each other stood, and in time we became very close personal friends. We buried the hatchet and went on.

Another traumatic case that I took care of involved a young man sitting on the side of a speeding boat instead of sitting in the boat. He was making a turn when he hit a wave and was thrown from the boat. The boat circled, and when he came up, the boat ran over him. As a result, he sustained several deep lacerations from the boat propellor to his back, arm, and chest. He was rescued and brought to the hospital, where his wounds were repaired. He recovered nicely, but the moral of the story is: "Don't ride on the side of a speeding boat."

In the practice of medicine, you run into some very difficult people. By that I mean difficult or almost impossible to get along with. One such patient was Brad (not his real name), who came into the emergency room after sustaining a gunshot wound to the abdomen by the local police. Brad was a bad actor, having been in trouble with the law on numerous previous occasions.

This episode started when Brad decided to enter a local clothing business through a ventilator on the roof of the building at night after closing. Some call it burglary, but he said he was only visiting. The burglar alarm went off, alerting local police of an illegal entry. When the officers arrived, he was caught leaving the roof with clothes on that he had taken from the store. The tags were still on the clothes. He tried to escape by running off, and paid no attention to the warnings by the police to stop. With that, a policeman shot him, and that brought him to his knees. He was then taken to the emergency room. The stolen coat he was wearing had a bullet hole of entry on one side, and an exit wound on the other side, as it had gone through the abdomen. He had been caught red handed.

When I saw him, I did not know the extent of his injuries, but I knew that he had serious injuries and that the bullet had penetrated the abdomen. He was prepared for surgery. Upon exploration, it was found that he had sustained a through-and-through gunshot wound of the liver, colon, stomach, small bowel, and spleen. He also had damage to his pancreas.

The abdomen contained approximately 1500 ccs. of blood that was evacuated so that the injuries could be identified. The spleen was removed, the perforations in the liver, colon, small bowel, and stomach were repaired, and drains were placed next to the liver and pancreas. He had a very bad injury. The surgery went well, and after a couple of days in intensive care, he was sent to the surgery ward.

There he really showed himself. The nurses told me that they were unable to handle him. He pulled out his levine tube, which is very necessary to keep pressure off the recent suture lines on the bowel in his abdomen. He pulled out his IVs, which were necessary to keep him hydrated, keep his electrolytes in balance, and give him antibiotics. He cursed at the nurses, spat at them, turned over his water on purpose, and in general made a real pain of himself. He also was demanding pain medication every two to three hours. The nurses were at their wits' end, and I wasn't about to let him destroy my surgery. I had too much invested in him. I told them not to worry. "Just leave him to me, and I will take care of the problem."

I very calmly spoke to him as he cussed me out, and I said to him, "Brad, let me tell you how this game is played; your behavior has been atrocious, and until it changes, there will be no more pain medication for you."

He said, "You can't do that; you're a doctor."

I said, "Just watch me."

With that I turned to the nurses and told them that he was absolutely not to receive any pain medication under any circumstances, no matter how much he complained. This was very hard for the nurses to do, but I was adamant and told them to watch and see what happened. He went the rest of the day and night with nothing for pain, and when I came in the next day, he was begging for pain medication. He spoke to me with great respect (as much as he was able to) and swore that he would behave, and no longer give the nurses a hard time.

I said "Okay, I will give you one more chance, but if you misbehave, it's all over."

From then on, Brad began to understand the program, and became a model patient. He recovered from the extensive surgery and was then transferred to prison, where he was going to pay his debt to society. I think he did a little growing up in the process.

One night I was called on to see a young man who had been involved in an automobile accident. While driving with his arm propped up in the open car window. He came around a curve at too great a speed. The car went through some trees, and he tore a hole in his left upper arm. The tear went to the bone, and almost completely severed the brachial artery (main vessel to the arm and hand). He had no pulse in the wrist, and the hand was turning blue.

He was taken to the OR, where the artery was reconstructed, which reestablished circulation, and he then had a pulse once again in his wrist. The young man was very lucky. We saved his arm. Every time I go by that curve (which is quite often), I think of that patient.

Chapter Sixteen
Interesting Experiences

With the passage of time, our area grew quite rapidly, and the need for hospital beds increased. The original 25-bed-Hill Burton Hospital increased in size to meet the needs of the community. It seemed as though the hospital was in continuous expansion. From the original through three expansions it grew to over 100 beds. Then in 1974 an entirely new Humana Hospital was built north of the old site. This was an exciting time for the community, and especially the medical staff. The new hospital had originally 230 beds with upgrades in all of the various departments. There was an increase in the number of operating rooms, delivery rooms, radiology rooms, and emergency rooms, and an increase in space in the departments of pathology, physical therapy, respiratory therapy, psychiatric care, and administration.

As the hospital grew, so did the medical community. There was an influx of doctors in various specialties. Instead of just having a small group of physicians on call to cover the emergency room, the hospital hired emergency-room physicians. After being the only board-certified surgeon in the county for 16 years, I was happy to see a young, very capable, board-eligible and later board-certified surgeon join the community. David Burkland and I worked well together. After years of working together for so long, we could almost anticipate the other's next move in the procedures. It was a great relationship, we had mutual respect for each other, and we have been close friends to this day.

In the practice of surgery many procedures are routine and can be performed with ease. For some reason, these procedures don't seem to stand out in your memory, but the cases that are difficult you never forget. One such case in which I was the surgeon and Dave assisted me was on a patient who came to the hospital with an intestinal obstruction of the small bowel.

Her past history was important. As a child she had received a gunshot wound in the abdomen. I anticipated that her obstruction was secondary to adhesions from her earlier gunshot wound. That was the case, and she must have had extensive peritonitis to have formed adhesions as numerous and dense as those we encountered. In the past I have operated on many patients with intestinal obstruction, but in all of my years of practice, I have never encountered adhesions as dense or as difficult to remove as those in this patient. We both still remember this case as the worst adhesions we had ever seen. Usually adhesions form for various reasons, including previous surgery, gunshot wounds, appendicitis, peritonitis, and other inflammatory causes. They can usually be freed up by blunt and sharp dissection, using caution to prevent injury to the bowel or other surrounding structures. In this case, her adhesions were so dense that an aggressive attack on her adhesions would cause damage to the surrounding small bowel.

Her bowel was literally glued together. After two hours of trying to free her obstruction, we were at our wits' end, and yet we had to clear up the obstruction if she was to survive. We traced the bowel to an area where we were able to bypass the obstruction. Sounds simple, but essentially we had to invent an operation to help her. She was a thin person anyway, and she had a pretty rough post-op course. She had to be put on hyperalimentation IV until we felt secure enough to put her on oral feedings. She survived, and now, 25 years later, she is still in good health and runs her own restaurant.

One Sunday morning as I was making rounds, I was called to the pediatric ward as an emergency. "Stat" was the terminology used in a serious emergency, and it was necessary to get to an area as quickly as possible. I ran to the ward, where the nurses were in a panic. A three-year-old child with a respiratory condition had suddenly blocked off his airway. Whether it was a mucous plug, or edema was not known, but the airway was blocked, and he could not get any air in or out through his trachea. All the wards had tracheotomy sets available for just this kind of emergency. I opened the set, and all the instruments were available to be able to do a tracheotomy. I had no time to waste, and performed a tracheotomy (opening in the trachea or breathing tube). This immediately opened the airway, and then the child was able to get air in and out of his lungs. The tube was sutured in place, and he went on to recover.

It was a stressful situation, because this was the son of a friend of mine. Luckily I happened to be in the hospital when the emergency came up. It would have been difficult to face the parents if the result had not been successful.

During that time period, it was routine for doctors in the community who performed hysterectomies to take out the appendix at the same time as the surgery. It was listed on the operative report as an incidental appendectomy, meaning that the appendix theoretically was normal, and not diseased.

In one such case, a prominent lady in the community underwent a hysterectomy and appendectomy by one of the gynecologists. He was a very capable trained surgeon in Ob/Gyn. All was well until the pathology report came back two days later and revealed a low grade cancer of the appendix present in the specimen.

My friend, the Ob/Gyn doctor, called me in for an opinion, and I told him that there was no choice; we had to go back in and do a wide resection of the area involved, including part of the colon, part of the small bowel, and the surrounding tissues and lymph nodes. We took her back to the operating room and completed the procedure. She did very well; there was no sign of any residual tumor, she has had no recurrence, and she is alive and well 25 years later.

Surgery in the earlier days and even today is really a work of art. Careful dissection and gentle handling of tissues is very important. It makes a difference in how well the patient recovers. If a surgeon is not careful nor respectful of tissues, he might not experience a good result. Surgery cannot be rushed, and yet if done properly, does not take any extra time. I have worked with several very good surgeons in my training and learned some very valuable lessons. I learned that if you made each move a step in the procedure that you don't have to rush and the surgery will go by quickly. I've seen surgeons so unsure of themselves that they took forever to complete a case. Half of their time was spent devoted to uncertainty and blotting blood with a sponge instead of moving forward with the procedure.

Times have changed, and now staples and other gadgets are being used very effectively. They all work, but the end result is not as esthetically pleasing to me. I guess that I am old fashioned, but I took great pleasure in doing a meticulous bowel resection with individual sutures. It was more of a work of art. I think I inherited that compulsion from my mother, who was an excellent seamstress.

While practicing medicine, you have to find time for some relaxation and also to spend time with your family. In late spring and summer I would close my practice early (except for emergencies) so that I could go home and water ski with the kids. I lived in a home on a bayou, which was ideal for water skiing, and we kept a speedboat on a lift directly behind the house. When I came home (around four p.m.), we would get the boat down and take turns skiing until dark. We always had a crowd. I had three children from my first wife, and four that belonged to my second wife. Sometimes they were all there, and sometimes they were not. It didn't matter; we would ski with whomever showed up, and we also took turns ourselves. We all became very proficient skiers.

These kids became exceptional water skiers, and with our demands for safety, were able to handle the ski boat very well. They knew only two speeds though, wide open and stop. They had a lot of stamina, and often to get them to stop their runs and give someone else a chance, I had to stop the boat, and then they would sink into the water, and I could give someone else a chance to ski. They often brought along some of their friends. It was a lot of fun.

Back then, Cypress Gardens was the best-known place in Florida for water skiing and trick skiing. Barefoot skiing was unknown until sometime later. In barefoot skiing, the skier gets up on one ski, the boat picks up speed, the skier puts one foot in the water to be used as a ski, and when positioned, he drops off his one ski, puts the other foot in the water, and is then skiing on just the soles of his feet. (It helps to have big feet.)

These kids became so good that they were able to "barefoot ski" for many miles. It was not unusual to have four boys (in their teens) skiing behind a boat, and all of them skiing barefoot all at one time. What was so unusual was that they were doing this before they started barefoot skiing at cypress gardens.

Later someone organized a ski show that was put on in the evenings where they did all kinds of stunts. The ski show was held behind the Sea Gull Restaurant. They had trick skiing, barefoot skiing, jumps over a pavilion, skiers stacked on each other forming a pyramid, and other stunts. Naturally our kids had to be a part of the show, and they did this for years.

Unfortunately, at that age they sometimes get involved with watching the skiers being pulled behind the boat, and forget to look where they are going while driving the boat. In general they are safe drivers, but sometimes they fail to use good judgement. One such episode happened one day when the kids were water skiing behind my house, and I was working.

The driver of the boat (son of a good friend of mine), was driving and looking back at the skiers that he was pulling, when he hit a dock at about thirty miles an hour. It flipped him over the dock, unconscious, and into the water. The crash smashed the front of the boat, and the people he was pulling swam to him, rescued him, and brought him to my home.

I received a call from home, while at the hospital, and they gave me the message that there had been a boating accident behind my house, and that they were bringing the body to the hospital. My heart sank. I didn't know who was injured, how severely, or if he was still alive. When they arrived at the hospital, I found out that it was the son of a friend of mine. He was alive and groggy. He had incurred numerous lacerations of his face and torso. It is a wonder that he wasn't killed.

In the emergency room, I cleaned his wounds and began to sew him back together. In the meantime, my friend arrived, and wanted to watch me sew up the lacerations on his son, and I foolishly let him watch. In a few minutes, he became very quiet, and when I looked around at him, he was as pale as a ghost. I said, "Get him out of here, or when he faints, I'll have someone else to sew up." All in all it was an exciting day, but the patient recovered and lived to ski another day.

Over the years we wore out several ski boats. They were put to good use, and we used them a lot. One year, my next door neighbor, Warren Taylor, called me and said, "Let's go water skiing."

I said "Okay, where are we going?"

He said "Let's ski to Navarre and back."

I said, "Are you crazy? That's fifty miles." Well, he shamed me into it, and we skied there and back without stopping. It took almost two hours, and neither of us would give in and quit. We finally made it home, totally exhausted.

Another time, I skied on a slalom (one ski) from Panama City through the intercoastal waterway, halfway across Choctawhatchee Bay, before I gave it up because of the rough water. That was about forty miles. I look back to fond memories of some of those adventures I had when I was younger and had more stamina. I no longer participate in the water sports, but I still enjoy living in this area and enjoy the great views of the bay and the gulf. It is a great place to live and raise kids.

Chapter Seventeen
Gall Bladder Surgery

The practice of surgery and the results from it are not just a simple issue. Some one can say that I just had surgery, and it sounds so simple, but it has many ramifications. First of all, why would a physician in training decide to specialize in surgery? It takes several components of a doctor's personality to be suited to a career in surgery. A good background in anatomy, physiology, biochemistry, pharmacology, and many other fields are essential prior to choosing this field.

There are good surgeons and not-so-good surgeons. Aside from the education, a good surgeon is usually a neat and compulsive individual. He must be caring and conscientious. He must be an individual who stays calm and doesn't come unglued when things do not go as planned. He must be aggressive and without fear. Imagine going into a patient who has sustained a gunshot wound of the abdomen and not knowing what to expect. He must be prepared to take care of any injury without panic. He must be prepared to take care of unusual circumstances not always described in the text books. He must be meticulous and treat tissues with respect. A patient with less tissue trauma heals sooner than one who has to overcome not only his injury, but also gross handling of tissues resulting in more tissue trauma.

Good judgement is essential. There are times when a surgeon can go ahead with a procedure, but there are also times when the surgeon has to back off or lose the patient on the operating table. Nothing is worse. He or she is not God, and in some cases, especially when dealing with cancer patients, not backing off and using good judgement can result in intractable, uncontrolled hemorrhage and death. Another area of good judgement is in deciding, after seeing a patient, when to operate and when not to operate. Surgery heals many problems, but is not a cure all in every case.

Deciding to become a surgeon is a very important decision. Taking a person's life in your hands on a daily basis is not to be taken lightly. There is nothing worse than having things go badly, and not necessarily the surgeon's fault, and having to go out and tell a parent or husband or wife that their loved one died during the procedure. Fortunately, this is a rare occurrence, but it will happen to anyone doing surgery over a number of years.

I will go through a gall bladder removal procedure to show what usually happens in the operating room. There are many different types of surgery, but this is just one example.

First of all, the operating room must be prepared so that there is relative sterility. I say "relative" because it is impossible to completely sterilize an operating room. You can sterilize instruments, gowns, sheets, etc., but you cannot sterilize the floor or shoes. Sometimes bacteria can be introduced into an operating room through air conditioning ducts. In spite of all of this, the operating room is relatively sterile.

The patient is brought in, put on the operating table, and prepared for surgery. The anesthesiologist, who has previously seen the patient, starts an IV and initiates anesthesia, followed usually by insertion of an endotracheal tube into the patient's trachea to have positive control of breathing. At that time, the abdomen is prepared, using various antiseptic materials. A favorite in my experience was betadyne, used before putting drapes on the patient. At that point, the surgeon comes in, after scrubbing his hands and forearms, and puts on a gown and gloves.

The incision for removal of the gall bladder is made below the rib cage on the right side of the patient. It is usually four-to-six inches long, depending on the size of the patient.

The incision is made through the abdominal wall. Bleeding has to be controlled by hemostats and ties, or a cautery, and the abdomen is opened. The gall bladder is then located and carefully dissected out of its bed in the bottom of the liver. The cystic artery (artery to the gall bladder) and cystic duct (duct from the gallbladder to the common bile duct), have to be carefully identified and tied off before removal of the gall bladder. Cholangiograms are then taken to be sure that no stones are left in the common bile duct. After removal of the gallbladder, the edges of the gall bladder bed are sutured, and drains are placed in the area and brought out through a separate incision (stab wound), and the abdomen is then closed in layers. Drains are usually necessary because blood or bile can drain from the raw undersurface of the liver. Drains come out in a few days, and then the sutures are removed.

Today endoscopy can be used in most cases to remove the gallbladder. This eliminates the need for an incision, pain is much less, and recovery time is shortened. The operative field is displayed on a television monitor, and fluoroscopy can be readily used to visualize the common bile duct, eliminating the need to drag a portable x-ray machine in and out of the operating room, another advantage of modern medicine! In my time, this option was not available.

I recall two other cases involving gall bladder surgery which I will now relate. One of them happened to the mother of one of my best friends, an attorney. We used to enjoy snow skiing in Colorado in the wintertime. My friend and I were gone together for a week to enjoy this sport, and when we came back to town, we found out that his mother, who had gallstones, had been operated on by one of the local general practitioners to remove her gall bladder.

One of my pet peeves when I arrived in Fort Walton Beach was having non-qualified doctors doing procedures that were beyond their ability. This case really taught this doctor a lesson he would never forget. When I returned to town, this doctor asked me to see my friend's mother in consultation. I agreed, and when I saw her, I saw that she was draining copious amounts of bile from around a T-tube that had been inserted in her common bile duct (bile duct from the liver to the small bowel) at the time of surgery. He said, "I think I'll just pull out this T tube."

I said, "Absolutely not! Let's get an x-ray by injecting dye into this tube that led to her common bile duct to see what she has."

He agreed, and we did exactly that. The x-ray showed that she had seven large gall stones left in her common bile duct. Had he pulled out the tube, she would have drained until her death.

She was about seventy-five years old at the time but had been in good health other than her gall-bladder disease. He asked me, "What shall we do?"

I told him that she needed surgery to remove all of the remaining stones as soon as possible, and he agreed and asked me to do the surgery. My friend, the attorney, was in complete agreement.

We took her to surgery the next day and found that he had removed the gall bladder and made an unsuccessful attempt to explore her common bile duct. He did remove a few stones, but seven were left in the duct. It was an inadequate exploration. In addition, he used cat gut to close the large opening he had made in the common bile duct. This is an absolute no, no, because the bile will absorb the cat-gut suture and will leave the duct wide open. A non-absorbable suture must be used in this area. I explored the common bile duct, removed the remaining stones, and closed the duct with silk sutures that are non-absorbable. I put in a new T-tube to be left in place until the duct had healed. It was removed several weeks later, and she recovered beautifully. She lived to the ripe old age of 93.

After this, my friend, (the doctor), did no more gall bladder surgery. I told him that if he were to get into a situation beyond his knowledge to call me. I would help him out of a jam at no charge to him or the patient, but please don't do any more of this kind of surgery. He never did. He learned his lesson.

Chapter Eighteen
More Patient Stories

Granny Boswell was a patient that I saw from time to time for various problems. She was slightly obese and had lost both of her feet and the lower third of her legs as a child from "bone infection." No one really knows for sure what the real cause was. At home, she got around on her hands and knees, and when she went out she used a wheelchair. She hadn't walked in years.

One day she came in to see me, and I thought, *Wouldn't it be wonderful if this patient could walk again?* I did some research on prosthesies and felt that I could shape what was left of her legs to fit into a prosthesis. I approached her on the subject, and she was elated at the prospect of being able to walk again.

I made her no promises, but I told her that I would try to make this happen. First, the legs had to be shaped to fit an artificial limb, and after this was accomplished and healed, she was fitted for a prosthesis for each leg. With physical therapy she slowly began to take some steps. In time, she gained strength and was able to walk with a cane. She was a very religious person, and she wanted to be able to walk down the aisle at the church. She planned for that day, and it finally happened. She took that walk before people in her church that had never seen her walk. It created quite a sensation. Her church members thought they had seen a miracle. I received no payment for this, nor did I expect any. My gratification was in seeing how happy this lady, her family, and I were at the results. It was a very gratifying experience.

Another satisfying experience was about a patient that needed surgery but could not afford it. She was not old enough for Medicare, not eligible for Medicaid, and could not afford health insurance. She was referred to me by a local physician who had ordered x-rays and found that she had gall stones, which were symptomatic. She had several attacks, but the patient put off the surgery because she couldn't afford it.

I agreed after reviewing her history and x-rays that she needed to have her gallbladder removed and told her so. She stopped me there. She said, "Doctor, I know that I need the surgery, but I cannot afford to pay your usual fee."

I never asked a new patient how they would pay for their surgery.

My criteria was whether or not the patient needed the surgery, and if they could not afford it, I would waive my fee. My response to her was that I was willing to do the surgery and charge no fee.

She was proud, and said "No, I can't pay your usual fee, but I want to pay something!"

I said, "Okay, what do you want to pay?" My usual fee at the time was $350 dollars for gallbladder surgery.

She said, "I can afford to pay $75 dollars, if you can give me time to pay."

I said, "Fine, how do you want to pay?"

She said, "I can pay five dollars a month if that's okay."

I told her again that I was willing to do this surgery for free, but she said, "No, I have my pride and want to pay what I can."

I was happy to agree. I did the surgery, and she preserved her feelings of pride and self esteem. This was a very satisfying and pleasant experience for me to deal with such an honorable patient. She kept her word, and over a period of time she paid it all off.

In the days before there was a plastic surgeon in this area, I was often called on to do emergency repairs after an accident. One such case comes to mind when I was called to the emergency room to see a victim of an automobile accident who had facial injuries. There was a prison camp twelve miles north of town. A prisoner broke out, stole the warden's car, and hit someone head on as he left the prison camp and entered the main highway. His face was a mess: his nose was split, and his cheeks were torn open and were just flaps. He had trouble breathing because of blood going down his trachea. It was the worst facial injury that I had ever seen. It was as if his face had exploded. Nevertheless, it was my duty to put him back together, so I proceeded to clean the wounds, freshen the edges, trim off damaged skin, stop the bleeding, and sew him back together. It took quite awhile and a lot of care, but when I finished he had a face that didn't look too bad.

Occasionally you see a patient with an acute abdomen and signs of peritonitis, but you have difficulty making a diagnosis. Any surgeon would like to have a presumptive diagnosis before doing surgery, but this is not always possible. The surgeon is left with a decision, and often the decision is to explore the abdomen rather than risk the patient's life by not taking care of the problem that is causing the peritonitis. Some of the unusual problems that I have seen are toothpick perforations of the small bowel with leakage, and also fishbone perforations with leakage. I've seen vascular insufficiency to the bowel with a segment of gangrene present. I've seen adhesions causing obstruction with damage to the small bowel and subsequent peritonitis. Diverticulitis with abcess formation, or meckels diverticulitis can also cause peritonitis and bleeding. Gangrenous bowel in a hernia is another serious condition that requires immediate surgery. There are other conditions that also require surgery, including acute appendicitis acute gall bladder disease, injuries following an auto accident, and ruptured spleen. There are others, but these are the most common. A surgeon must be prepared to take care of any of these problems.

Not all surgery is done as an emergency; most surgeries are routine but varied. Some of the cases that I did were simple, and others were more complicated. Splenectomy, hernia repair, cholecystectomies, thyroidectomies, tonsillectomies, vein strippings, small bowel resections, skin grafts, and hysterectomies are routine. When you get into pulmonary surgery, esophageal resections, gastric surgery, hiatal hernia repair, common duct exploration, open hip fractures, pancreatic surgery, and colon surgery, it becomes a little more complicated.

Cancer surgery must be done very carefully to keep from spreading tumor cells. In this type of surgery, with early diagnosis and treatment, the cure rate can be fairly high depending on the tumor type that you are treating. That makes it all worthwhile.

Open orthopedics with the use of screws, plates, and other devices can be a very gratifying type of surgery. There was no orthopedic surgeon in Fort Walton Beach when I arrived, and having had orthopedic training in my residency I was able to do a considerable amount of that kind of work. It satisfies ones sense of logic and order to align the bones and then put screws or plates over the fracture to hold it in place. I felt like a sophisticated carpenter. It can be very precise.

In most operations, the use of transfusions for blood loss is unnecessary. But there are times when the use of blood for replacement is critical. It sometimes becomes a matter of life and death. Certain religious groups, for example, Jehovah's Witnesses, do not believe in receiving blood under any circumstances. Even in emergencies where blood replacement is necessary, they are willing to die from the loss of blood rather than take a transfusion.

You can imagine the difficult position in which this belief puts the surgeon. Many doctors refuse to take on a patient for surgery who tells them up front that they want no blood transfusions.

When I came to this area to practice, I was faced with this problem. I elected to do the surgery, and promised to not give a transfusion to any of these people that had this belief. As a result, I cornered the market on all of the people of this faith in and around this local area. They passed the word around, and naturally I had to be extremely cautious to prevent blood loss during surgery. Even though I did some fairly complex procedures, I never broke my promise nor lost any of these patients, and they were very appreciative.

Fort Walton Beach in the early days had a small black population centered around Germany Drive. There was a bar called Silver Inn, and it was kept busy on Saturday nights with people relaxing. I took care of many of our black residents that became involved in altercations at the Silver Inn Bar.

When it comes to medicine and surgery, there is no discrimination. White and black all look the same on the inside. The color of their skin never became an issue, and I gave them the best care that I could. One friend that really believed in me was Julius McKinnon. He was very popular in the community, but also managed to get into quite a few scrapes. I sewed him up several times, and one time had to open his chest after he had received a gunshot wound. He and I became very good friends. Because of the number of cases that I had done involving people they knew, they came up with a nickname for me. I was known as, "The Big Knife." I was pleased that they gave me this term of endearment and the respect that went with it. Julius later settled down and became a security guard at the local airport. He was a nice friend.

Acute appendicitis is a serious surgical emergency. If not treated, if it goes on to rupture, appendicitis can be life threatening. The diagnosis is easily made by physical examination and lab work. There is usually tenderness in the right lower quadrant of the abdomen associated with what is called rebound tenderness. What this means is that after pressing on the abdomen and releasing suddenly, there is acute pain in that area. It is a reflection of irritation of the peritoneum or inner lining of the abdomen being inflamed close to the appendix. The white blood cell count is usually elevated, and this helps to confirm the suspicion of appendicitis.

A famous New Orleans stripper who called herself "The Cat Girl" (Lillie Christeen) died of a ruptured appendix. Because she had a beautiful body and wanted no scars, she refused surgery. What a waste! Surgery is done when the symptoms are present. To ignore these signs is unacceptable because the consequences are so serious.

I had a five-year-old patient brought in by his mother with all of the signs and symptoms of acute appendicitis. After my examination, I told the mother that the child had acute appendicitis and needed to have surgery. She turned to her son and said, "Johnny, the doctor says that you have acute appendicitis and need to have surgery. What do you think? Do you want to have surgery?" I was appalled and told the mother that this child had no medical education, and was not capable nor mature enough to make this decision. This was not his decision to make. This child needed surgery, and if she didn't believe me, that she should get a second opinion, and that I would not take the responsibility of watching him get sicker. She then relented, and I took out Johnny's acute appendix, and he went home cured.

I could not believe that a mother in her right mind would ask a five-year-old child to make the decision if he wanted surgery. Crazy people!

Chapter Nineteen
Breast Cancer

The oldest record of breast cancer dates back to 1600 B.C. According to information found on an ancient papyrus, cauterization was one of the only earlier treatments for this disease. Hippocrates in 460 A.D. was able to distinguish between most benign and malignant tumors of the breast. He, along with many others of his period, considered breast cancer incurable, but small, benign breast tumors were amenable to surgical excision.

In 1894, two physicians, Halstead and Myer, independently announced their own surgical procedures for the treatment of breast cancer. They both described local control of the disease by en bloc radical mastectomy, which included total removal of the affected breast, total axillary lymph node dissection, and removal of the pectoralis major and minor muscles. They based their opinion on the medical thinking at that time, that cure can only be achieved by the local removal of tumor along with adjacent healthy tissue. A ten-year survival rate of 34% was realized, which at the time was clearly superior to other efforts. Radical mastectomy, according to Halstead, brought out a new era and approach to breast-cancer treatment. His classical radical mastectomy was the treatment of choice for many years.

Breast cancer is the most common malignant tumor among women. In many countries it is the leading cause of death from malignant diseases among women. In most countries of the world, incidence and mortality increases with age, the highest rate being among women over the age of 85, where the incidence is over 350 cases per 100,000. Breast cancer occurs 100 times more often in women than in men. Breast cancer family history is important for the first generation of female family members. That is, mother, daughter, and sister. Women whose mothers had bilateral breast cancer before menopause carry the highest risk. They have a nine-times higher risk than other women.

Radiation exposure increases the risk of breast cancer development. For example, the A bomb dropped on Hiroshima and Nagasaki significantly increased the risk of breast cancer in that region over the next 20-year period.

There has been a gradual improvement in the treatment of localized breast cancer. Initially incurable, treatment of breast cancer has not only improved cure rates, but also allowed women to keep their breasts.

At the turn of the century, there was no known cure for breast cancer. The best treatment of the time was Dr. Halstead's radical mastectomy. This surgery, as all-encompassing as it sounds today, was a dramatic step forward in showing that breast cancer is potentially curable.

The first real modification to the surgery came in the late 1950s. At this time, the breast was removed, along with the regional lymph nodes, but the pectoral muscles were left, creating a more cosmetic result. This was known as the modified radical mastectomy. The cure rates were later proven to be identical to the Halstead radical, but with a dramatic improvement in appearance and a decrease in complications. There was a decrease in the incidence of lymphedema (arm swelling) along with improved arm strength and mobility. The cosmetic improvement gave women the ability to wear lower-cut blouses and short sleeves. This was a huge improvement over the old techniques.

Plastic reconstructive surgery in the early 1960s saw the introduction of plastic surgical breast reconstruction. Cosmetics became a very important factor, as physicians became aware of the psychologic impact mastectomy was having on breast-cancer survivors. Lumpectomy, (breast preserving surgery) was introduced in the mid 1960s. Accepting for the first time that radiation could cure smaller-sized cancers, physicians combined "limited" surgery with breast radiation to preserve the breast. The procedure is known as "lumpectomy," "quadrant resection," "wedge resection," and "wide local excision." This surgery is followed by radiation to the breast. Again, long-term studies showed equivalent cure rates but dramatically better acceptance of the newer treatment by women. Many variations have been developed since then, altering the course of radiation in treatment.

Breast cancer treatment has become increasingly sophisticated over the last fifty years, and from early cure rates of 34%, surgeons have achieved cure rates of 93% (no evidence of disease for 12 to 15 years). Doctors have made a huge step forward in the treatment of this disease.

Over a period of thirty years, I had the privilege of not only performing many of these surgeries on patients with cancer of the breast, I was also able to participate in the improvements that came along during that time. I saw the cure rates improve and the overall appreciation by patients who were diagnosed with breast cancer.

Mammography was a newer procedure that was used for the early detection of cancer of the breast. It's not 100% accurate, but that procedure, along with physical examination, and if necessary biopsy, is very helpful in the early diagnosis and treatment of breast malignancies. Very often, clinical impression, along with x-ray studies, is very important in making a decision.

I remember, sadly, one patient that I saw in the office who had a small lump in one of her breasts. I recommended a biopsy, but she and her husband were reluctant to go ahead with the biopsy. They elected to go to Pensacola for a mammography and a second opinion. This procedure was new at the time, and as I said before, is not 100% accurate, being based on the determination of the radiologist reading the mammography. Her mammography showed no suspicious areas and was interpreted as normal, so she and her husband were relieved.

Her husband was a physician, and it was hard to convince him, but I told her and her husband that I didn't care what the mammogram showed, she had a lump in her breast, and it needed to be biopsied. In spite of my best efforts to convince them, they elected to believe the mammography and not have the breast biopsied.

They were gone out of town for several months, and when they returned she came back to see me. The small lump that I had felt (one-two cms.) had grown to about three inches in diameter. At that time she submitted to biopsy with frozen section, and it proved to be an aggressive breast malignancy. Radical mastectomy was performed with axillary node dissection. Several of these nodes were positive for malignancy. She received chemotherapy and radiation therapy to no avail, and was dead one year later. I was devastated. These were very close personal friends, and I think back and wonder if there might have been any way that I could have convinced them earlier to have gotten a biopsy, and if so, would the results have been any different.

I saw a patient in my office one day with one of the worst breast cancers that I had ever seen, and I have seen quite a few. It was horrible. Half of the breast was eroded away. It was ulcerated and bleeding, and the smell from this necrotic breast was unbearable. It was quite a large breast. She was a charity patient and had waited to see a doctor because she thought that the Lord would heal her. As it became worse, she realized that it wasn't going to improve, so she decided to come in.

At this time, there was a tumor clinic in Pensacola that took care of many difficult cases, most of which were people that could not afford hospital or medical care. They had on their staff all kinds of specialists to treat the various difficult problems that they had to face. I thought that this would be an ideal patient for the tumor clinic to tackle, since this was a rather extreme case, so I sent her to the tumor clinic for evaluation and treatment. When they saw her, they decided that I should take care of her myself, so they called me and told me so. They just didn't want to tackle it. The patient needed care, so I scheduled her for surgery. The smell was so bad that every one in the operating room soaked their mask with oil of wintergreen so that we could tolerate the smell. The tumor was so large that I had to remove the breast and a very large area around it to give me a good margin around the malignancy. It turned out to be a very low-grade malignancy, and she didn't even have any lymph nodes positive for cancer. That was quite a surprise when we found out after the pathologist had a chance to examine the surgical specimen. I had to do a fairly large skin graft to close the surgical incision. I saw her in the office several times after her discharge from the hospital, and she healed surprisingly well. After all that, believe it or not, I think she had a good chance of being cured of her cancer. I let my colleagues in Pensacola know about my findings, and they were quite surprised and impressed, and pleased that they didn't have to tackle that piece of surgery. She was a very grateful and happy patient.

I remember very well, a patient, a nurse who I new very well, who came in to see me for a lump in the breast. She was quite frightened, which most of these patients are, and this reaction is understandable. We discussed the problem. I recommended immediate biopsy, frozen section, and if the report showed that the lump was malignant, then radical mastectomy was the treatment of choice. She said that she would think about what I told her and then decide what to do. She was a young, attractive lady.

The next thing I knew was that she decided to go to Pensacola to have her surgery. It was the patient's option, and I had no problem with her decision. Some months later, I heard that she had developed metastasis, and within one year of her surgery, she had died. Looking back, I was very sad that she passed away, but I was very happy that I was not the surgeon that did her surgery and would have to live with the consequences. Sometimes you just get lucky and avoid heartache.

Surgery of the breast for cancer, if found early, carries a fairly high cure rate. Today, there are numerous ways to treat malignancies of the breast, and much depends on the kind of cancer, how early it is found, and various other factors.

Chapter Twenty
Strange Tales

Bankers can be unusual people, but they are also human at times. I remember an episode with one of the local bankers that is worth recalling. I had a loan with this bank, and had many dealings with the bank in the past. The interest rate was quite high, so I decided to refinance my loan for a lower rate with another banking institution. When I approached the bank to pay off the loan, they decided to add a penalty for early payoff. That's fine as long as the interest rate is within legal limits.

At the time in Florida, the legal limit for this particular type of loan was 10%. Anything higher than this was considered usury (illegal, and above the legal lending limit). I pointed this out, but they were not interested in my interpretation of the banking laws, and it was still to my advantage to pay off the loan, so I proceeded to do so. I also pointed out that what they were doing was illegal, and that I would remember this. I no longer did any business with this bank.

A few years later, this same banker came to my office to meet with me. He handed me a check for about $2000.00. I said, "What's this all about?"

He said that this was for the amount of the overcharge on the previously paid-off loan. It turned out that he needed his gall bladder removed, and his son needed a hernia repair. He wanted to make things right with me before asking me to do surgery on him or his son.

I accepted the check and thanked him and said, "It takes a big man to admit that he is wrong." Not that I would treat him any different from any other patient coming in for surgery, but he wasn't going to take that chance, especially since he had done me wrong in the past. He made things right before having his surgery. The operations went well on both him and his son, and we remained friends long thereafter.

We took turns being on call in the emergency room, and we frequently ran into some unusual problems. One such problem that came in was where a patient came in with a complaint that he had a vibrator lodged inside his rectum, and he couldn't get it out.

It's not easy to pull a vibrator or a coke bottle (which I have seen also) out of a rectum. You can get hold of it with an instrument, and pull to your heart's content, and you will not be able to budge it. The colon collapses around it as you pull, forms a vacuum behind it, and no matter how hard you pull, it just will not move. The secret to removing it is to insert a catheter past it in the colon, which lets air in behind it, and then it slips out very easily. It breaks down the vacuum. By doing this I was able to remove the vibrator with no problem.

Once wasn't enough. I had to be subjected to this embarrassing problem twice. I sure did take a lot of teasing because of these episodes. I was known as the vibrator-extraction expert. My colleagues asked me in jest if I really had only been asked by the patient to take out the vibrator, or to only change the batteries. One of these patients, when asked how the vibrator got in there, said that he fell on it. Sure! As if I would believe that.

I saw a five-year-old boy in the emergency room one day with an acute abdomen. His lower abdomen was very tender, and he had signs of peritonitis. It was difficult to get a history on him from his parents, but it finally came out that he was in the shower, and as he came out of the shower, he slipped and fell on a plunger that was in the bathroom. The plunger went into his rectum, and he suffered severe pain after that. Not a very believable story, but his parents insisted that it was true.

He was taken to surgery, and I found a tear in his colon. Apparently, the plunger went into the rectum far enough that it reached the sigmoid colon and went through it. The injury was repaired, and he recovered, but I never did find out if the story was true. I suspect though that this may have been an early case of sexual abuse on a child, but I could never prove it.

One other story that I must tell to show some of the aggravations in medical practice happened to a close friend of mine, a family practitioner and a very competent physician. He performed a rectal examination on a patient of his as part of a routine physical examination. His fee for the physical, including the rectal examination was $15.00. The patient complained to the doctor that the fee was too high. My friend then asked him what he would charge for sticking his finger up some stranger's ass?

He said, "I just wouldn't do that."

My friend then said, "Okay, then pay me."

That settled that problem. This doctor, Bernard Russell, was a classmate of mine, and we worked together for fifty years. He has been a close personal friend, and I appreciate his talents and friendship to this day.

The practice of medicine is usually intense, requiring thought, concentration, and attention to details and the needs of patients. Occasionally amusing situations arise to allow you to laugh at yourself and come back to reality. One such event happened to me one night when a close friend of mine, Dr. Parker, woke me up during the middle of the night. We had worked together on many patients in the past and respected each other's opinion.

When he called me at night, it was usually a serious and necessary call. This night, he woke me out of a sound sleep and told me about a patient that had been burned. Being still asleep, I asked the dumb question, "What did she get burned with?"

There was a long pause, and he said, "A house." With that, I woke up and realized what was going on, and I said, "Okay, I'll be right there," so I dressed and responded. I took a lot of kidding by him and others over my response and his answer.

While in the practice of medicine, a doctor has to be constantly on the alert for allergic reactions. The patient, before being given any medication or injections is always asked if he or she has any allergy to any medications. The patient may not always know if he has any allergies, or they may have a reaction to a medication that they have never received but that when given can cause a reaction.

I had this happen to me in my office one day while doing a minor procedure. Office surgery is limited to fairly simple procedures that can be performed under local anesthesia, and it is rare to have a reaction. I had a patient who had come into the office for a vasectomy. That usually is a very simple procedure, done using local anesthesia.

The patient was prepared for the surgery, and the area was shaved, and painted with an antiseptic solution. I injected the area where the incision was to be made with Novocaine, which was the local anesthetic, and within minutes, the patient had a reaction and passed out. Fortunately, we always had drugs on hand to take care of any emergency that might arise. This was one of them. I immediately injected an adrenaline solution, and the patient responded and was once again alert. It was an exciting episode for both the patient and me. In 25 years of practice, this was the only time that I had ever seen a reaction to local anesthesia, and it was somewhat frightening. Naturally the surgery was then cancelled.

Another problem that rarely occurs is a transfusion reaction after blood has been given. This can be an early or late manifestation. I had a patient who had cancer of the rectum that I took to surgery. In a case like this, the procedure of choice is to perform an abdominoperineal resection. The surgeon enters the abdomen and releases the lower colon from its blood supply and the surrounding tissues. The rectum is then dissected away from under the bladder and the pelvis, and a colostomy is performed. The pelvis is then covered with abdominal lining (peritoneum) and the terminal colon is then removed from below, including the rectal area.

This is an extensive piece of surgery and almost always requires blood transfusion for the replacement of blood lost during the long procedure. It is performed with the hope of curing a cancer of the rectum, and usually the results are quite good. In this case it was a small malignancy, and the chances of a cure were excellent. After removing the specimen from below, there is usually some bleeding from the area of dissection in the pelvis, which is usually controlled by the use of a cautery. Pressure packs are then used to compress the bleeders, which come through the bony pelvis.

In this case, she developed a hemolytic reaction, in that the blood would no longer clot. After all of our efforts, including many units of blood, platelets and other medications, we couldn't control the bleeding, and she succumbed to the blood dyscrasia and died on the operating table. This was a heartbreaker, but there was nothing else that we could do. It is one of the unknowns in surgery. Her chances of cure from her cancer were excellent, but she was defeated by a bleeding abnormality that we were unable to control.

Shortly after I moved to Fort Walton Beach, for the most part, I was welcomed as the only surgeon in the area, but there were some that resented my intrusion into their area. One night while going to our favorite Italian restaurant, Perri's, a local attorney decided to verbally attack me, saying that doctors were bad, and that my fees were too high, and so on. I think he had taken on too much to drink.

I then told him that my highest fee ever was for a major case of a gunshot wound with multiple organ injuries and a long post-operative course, and that I had saved the patient's life. My fee for that was less than $1500.

Then he said in a boastful way that his highest fee was $20,000, and he said, "I saved his life also."

With that, I said, "Sure you did," and turned away and left him stammering.

I had a short, but interesting period of time when I became involved in local and state politics. Once was enough, though; it just wasn't for me. It happened that during a race for governor in the state of Florida in the 1960s. Politicians from both the Democratic and Republican parties were looking for physicians to head up the local political parties. A friend and I were chosen to represent each party. We reluctantly agreed, not really knowing what we were doing.

We had to organize the local campaigns, recruit helpers, and help in any way that we could to get our candidate elected. This also meant moderate monetary contributions, but this was all part of the game. My friend and I worked hard at our new duties, and it was a friendly, competitive effort. He represented Robert King High, and I represented Scott Kelly. It was a close race, and the competition was hot and heavy.

It turned out that his candidate won the race, and my candidate and I were the losers, temporarily. I did get my revenge, though. I don't know if it was the stress of campaigning, or just a coincidence, but my colleague, who was one of my very best friends, had developed a case of thrombosed hemorrhoids. One of these needed surgical incision and drainage. Now guess who had the pleasure of performing the dirty deed. I had my revenge, by sticking a knife in my opponents rectum, and now it was my turn to have the last laugh. It made for a good story.

A friend of mine, Jack Bernard, who had been in the Navy with me, found me on the Internet and called me at home, a few years ago, and left a message in which he said, "If this is the Gene Celano who was a Navy pilot, call me." I was tickled to hear from him, and I called him back and we later got together to tell what had happened to each of us over the last 57 years. We had both trained in F6F fighters at the Banana River Naval Air Station in Florida. It is now known as Patrick Air Force Base, at the space center at Cape Canaveral. I still have a picture of our group of six young ensigns posing in front of an F6F. We later went to sea together on the same carrier flying F8F Bearcats. We had a great reunion.

The first question he asked me was "How many surgeons do you know that have had one hundred carrier landings?"

I said, "To my knowledge only me."

He had a career in the insurance business, and I went on to medical school. He stopped flying after his discharge from the Navy, but I continued to fly in the Navy reserves, flying Corsairs for a period of time while I was going to Tulane in pre-med. Later as a civilian, I flew about eight different airplanes over the years, and accumulated 4000 hours of flight time. I finally gave it up, but I still miss it.

Chapter Twenty-One
Changes in Medical Practice

Early attempts at diagnosis of arterial disease were very primitive. Vascular surgery was in its infancy when I started residency training. We tried to diagnose arterial blockage in larger vessels by injecting radio-opaque dye into the vessel, and rapidly shooting an x-ray. You had to be quick to catch it. It wasn't much, but occasionally we could detect an obstruction or clot. These were usually caused by plaques and arteriosclerosis in the femoral or other arteries.

A patient would come in with sudden severe pain in the leg, then under local anesthesia, the blockage by clot would be removed, reestablishing circulation and relieving the pain. This is a far cry from the sophisticated procedures that are available in radiology today. There have been so many wonderful changes in the medical field.

Since I started private practice in 1960, many changes have come about in that relatively short period of time. In 1960, dialysis for kidney failure was in its infancy. In those days, if we had a patient in renal failure, dialysis was not available, and we used ringers solution, which is IV fluid, to irrigate the abdominal cavity. We would insert needles into the peritoneal cavity on one side, and allow it to flow through the abdomen to the other side where it was drained out. This was far from perfect, but it did help to reduce the blood urea nitrogen.

In patients with temporary renal shutdown, it helped the patient long enough that his own kidneys might begin to take over their own function. This procedure often had to be repeated and was a far cry from modern-day renal dialysis, but it was all we had at the time. Kidney dialysis was a remarkable improvement in the care of patients who had severe renal problems.

When I went through training, cataract surgery was being performed, but lens implants were not available. After cataract removal, the patient had to be fitted for glasses with lenses that were as thick as coke-bottle bottoms. After the surgery was performed, a patient had to lie flat on his back with sand bags placed on each side of the head after the surgery. This was to prevent any head movement that might cause possible separation of the sutures that had been placed in the eye. The patient had to stay that way for 10 days. Besides the discomfort, trouble urinating or having bowel movements, and blood clots in the legs added to the complications.

Today, what an improvement! The cataract can be removed and a lens put in place at the same time. The patient's stay in the hospital is one day or less, and he can then go home. Not only that, but after lens implant, vision is often returned to 20/20. Vein thrombosis is negligible, and often the surgery is done as an outpatient. What a marvelous improvement! Another miracle of modern medicine.

In the early 60s, open-heart surgery was unheard of except in institutions, and then it was being done almost on an experimental basis. Today, open-heart surgery is almost routinely done, and is being performed around the country with excellent results. Coronary artery bypass surgery has extended many patient's lives, mine included. In 1994, I underwent triple bypass surgery after chest discomfort, and diagnosis by coronary angiography. A friend of mine did my surgery, and when asked if I had any questions, all I had to say was, "Make sure your knife is sharp." I had an excellent result, and even after ten years, was able to go the limit on my stress tests.

My father was 49 years old when he died of a coronary occlusion. I guess that it ran in the family. We've come a long way. Hospital stay after that kind of extensive surgery is only four-five days. I'm still almost in disbelief when I think of how, with this remarkable surgery, they can stop your heart, put you on a heart/lung machine, and literally give you new coronary arteries. My hat's off to those very bright surgeons who made all of this possible. In Orlando, Florida, 2000 bypass procedures are performed each year, and many others are now being done around the state.

A relatively new procedure now being done is the implantation of "stents," stiff tube-like structures that keep arteries open and allow blood to flow through the vessels unobstructed. These can be placed in selected cases without having to open the chest. The technology is so good that this can be done with the help of the radiologist by inserting the stent into a major artery, manipulating it until it is in place in a coronary artery or other vessel, and then leaving it in place to allow blood to flow unobstructed. Clotting of stents used to be a problem, but now, the newer ones are medicated, which reduces the possibility of clotting.

Placement of arterial grafts is now commonplace; they are used to repair arterial blockages, or used to replace aortic or renal aneurysms. I recall a case that I was assisting on to repair an abdominal aortic aneurysm. The aneurysm was the size of a large grapefruit; this one was well overgrown, since any aneurysm larger than five cms. should come out to prevent rupture. This one was easily 15 cms., and while I was removing it from the surrounding tissues, it blew out. Wow! We stopped the bleeding by clamping the aorta, and when we were through with our dissection, we put in an aortic graft. This procedure today is common, and the results are good. In those days we were looking at 25% mortality with that kind of surgery. Today it's down to 3%. Another major advance in surgery.

Most strokes are caused by blockage or plaque in the carotid arteries in the neck. Today, many of these can be prevented. With newer techniques, the artery can be opened, clots or plaque removed, a stent inserted, and the vessel closed around it. This is a relatively safe and very useful procedure.

Surgery is now performed on "blue babies." These newborns are brought into the world with a defect between the chambers of the heart. It causes oxygenated blood to be mixed with unoxygenated blood. The result is that the baby, because of the mixture of the blood, has blue discoloration of its skin. The repair of this defect is almost a routine procedure, and the baby goes on to live out a normal life.

Surgery can be done to actually remove aneurisms of the cardiac musculature by removing the weak or diseased muscle and sewing the heart muscle back together. The patient is then left with a much stronger heart. Diseased heart valves caused by rheumatic fever in childhood can now be replaced. There are many other heart and vascular procedures that can be performed in addition to those that I have mentioned. Progress in the past forty years has been dramatic and continues to this day. Heart disease that was untreatable years ago can now be treated with medicine or surgery with relatively low mortality.

The advances in radiology are absolutely remarkable. Since 1960, MRIs, CT scans, mammographies, arteriograms, arthrograms, and other procedures have been developed. For example, in a patient suspected of having a ruptured spleen, in the early days, confirmation of the diagnosis was made by inserting a needle into the abdomen to detect the presence or absence of blood. This, along with decreasing hemoglobin and a tender or acute abdomen put the surgeon in a position where exploration was performed without a definitive diagnosis. Now, not only can the diagnosis of ruptured spleen be made radiologically and with CT scans, the severity and location of the tear can be made before exploration.

Magnetic resonance imaging or MRI is another remarkable tool the radiologist has. With this technique, areas that were impossible to examine can now be seen in detail. Based on the findings, exploration of these areas in many cases can be avoided, or information and be gathered that could be helpful at exploration.

Today, there are many sophisticated radiological studies performed routinely. Open-heart surgery with arterial bypass now is performed with full knowledge of what the status of the coronary arteries is before and after bypass surgery. A catheter is passed from the femoral artery to the heart, and dye is then injected into the coronary arteries, outlining the narrowing or occlusion. As the dye is injected, x-rays are taken, and the technology is so good that multiple x-rays can be taken very rapidly. With this information, the surgeon can determine if he needs to do bypass surgery or put in a stent to open the vessel. These are now being placed in the arteries under fluoroscopy by the radiologists, as non-invasive procedures, preventing opening the chest.

Recently, a new technique has been developed in which the somewhat risky arteriogram can be avoided. With the injection of opaque material into a vein, a CT scan can be done, and the coronary arteries visualized. Vascular surgery has come a long way in a short time.

Approximately 2/3 of colon malignancies are found within the length of a sigmoidoscope (25 cms. long). Sigmoidoscopy used to be performed very routinely, especially if a patient had bleeding from the rectum. The scope is non-flexible, approximately one inch in diameter, twenty-five cms. long, and very uncomfortable for the patient. Air is pumped into the colon to look for problems. Air expands the colon, and various lesions can be seen, such as polyps and or malignancies, diverticulitis, and bleeding.

This is no longer necessary since the advent of the fiberoptic technology in the colonoscope. The scope is much smaller in diameter than the sigmoidoscope, flexible, and can now be used to visualize the entire colon, take biopsies, stop bleeding, or remove polyps. The patient experiences much less discomfort, and the doctor can see the entire colon more easily. While seeing the whole colon, pictures of any lesions present can be taken. This procedure has proven to be very useful, especially in removing polyps and avoiding future colon cancers. Color photographs are taken of any area in the colon for the patient's information and for future reference. This is a significant improvement over the sigmoidoscope.

Hearing aids are another technological improvement that we have seen in the medical field. The patient, inside a soundproof booth, is asked to identify various sounds. This can also be done by the use of computers, testing each ear independently. The operator can vary the intensity of the sound, and the patient lets the operator know when the sound is heard.

After completion of the hearing test, a chart is made of the patient's range of hearing in the various sound levels, and compared to the expected normal range of hearing. Based on these findings, the patient can then be individually fitted for digital hearing aids of various types. Some of these are so small that they can be fitted into the ear canal. It provides quite an improvement in the quality of life.

Endoscopic surgery is a new technique where a surgeon can use an instrument to invade spaces that were not exposed before without an incision. This lessens the pain involved in the surgery, and shortens the amount of time it takes to recover from an incision. This surgery now can be performed to take out gallbladders, and at the same time, take x-rays of the common bile duct. These can be done without the difficulties we used to have. We used to have to use a portable x-ray machine, placing the film under the patient, removing it with difficulty, sending the film to radiology to be read by the radiologist, and then getting a report. It was cumbersome and time consuming. Today, with the modern equipment, the x-ray machine is a part of the operating room equipment, and it gives the surgeon the ability to immediately see what the common duct looks like under fluoroscopy and feel secure that no stones are left behind.

With the endoscope, the surgeon now also has the ability to resect a bowel, take out an appendix, fix a hernia, repair certain knee joint conditions such as a torn meniscus in the knee, and other procedures. The patient recovers sooner, and the hospital stay is shortened. In most cases, these procedures can be done as an outpatient in a surgery center and not even require hospitalization because there is less trauma to the tissues, recovery is quicker, and the infection rate in wounds is lowered.

Who would have thought in the early days that hip and knee joints could be replaced? These are now common procedures. The worn-out knee and hip joints are removed and replaced with titanium or ceramic implants. Results vary, but most patients can return to their normal activities after recovery from the surgery. It keeps a lot of patients out of wheelchairs.

A lot of progress has been made in the development of prostheses for replacement of lost limbs. Whereas, with the loss of a hand or lower arm previously, all that was available was a hook on the distal arm, now highly technical artificial limbs are available that can be used to replace the missing part. These artificial limbs can perform many functions previously not thought possible.

The use of the microscope or operating lenses by the surgeon has enabled him to do specialized surgery in various parts of the body. By enlarging the operative field, it makes it much easier to see vital structures. This has been especially helpful in opthalmology and otology, where the structures are small and hard to see just using the naked eye. For example, in patients with no hearing, tiny parts of the hearing mechanism can be surgically repaired or replaced and hearing is often restored.

Now surgery is being performed by robotics. This is being performed with increasing frequency in patients with cancer of the prostate. Whereas earlier techniques were very gross, with considerable bleeding and complications, robotic surgery has many advantages. One is the nerve-sparing technique. Prostatectomy patients can have several possible complications. One of them is incontinence and the need to wear a diaper after surgery. Another is the inability of the patient to have an erection, and impotence. Another is the significant blood loss from the old type of surgery. With robotic surgery, there is less tissue trauma, less bleeding, more nerve preservation, less impotence, and a shorter hospital stay. With robotic surgery, there is magnification on the operating field so that structures can be better visualized and be seen from all sides. This enables the operator to better control bleeding and is able to identify and preserve the nerves. It is a major advancement in this and other types of surgery. This represents quite an advancement in technology to be able to perform these delicate procedures.

Glaucoma can be arrested by surgical procedures designed to reduce pressure inside the eye. When the pressure is relieved, the damage to the retina stops or slows down, and the patient maintains present vision. Without these procedures, a patient would continue to lose vision and eventually become blind.

Operating lenses have enabled the surgeon to perform surgery on small blood vessels, such as those seen in coronary artery bypass, or in replacing a limb that has been severed. There are many cases in which a limb was severed, brought to the hospital, and reattached. To do this, the tiny vessels as well as nerves have to be sewn together with tiny sutures. Using magnification from the new technology makes this intricate surgery possible. Without a blood supply and nerve regeneration the replacement of a limb would not be possible.

Advances in discovery of new drugs has helped many patients to live a longer, fuller, more active lifestyle. Drug companies spend a considerable amount of money each year on research and development. This is money well spent. I remember very well when polio was an active disease, and many children suffered as a result. Charity hospital in New Orleans had a three-story building dedicated only for the care of polio victims. To see a patient doomed for life in an iron lung is a very sad picture. Their muscles of respiration were paralyzed, and without the iron lung, they could not survive. Many children were afflicted with this disease, and they were left with varying degrees of paralysis. As a physician or parent it was heartbreaking to see these children. Now since the discovery of the Salk vaccine, polio is almost non existent.

Many new vaccines are available today to prevent serious illnesses. Smallpox has essentially been eradicated. German Measles (rubella) is down to approximately 150 cases a year in the United States. It is practically gone. This type of measles is very serious in pregnant women. If a pregnant woman developed rubella in her first trimester, the effect on the newborn can be disastrous. Congenital defects, heart problems (blue babies), cataracts, glaucoma, deafness, stillbirths, abortion, and mental deficiencies are just some of the problems that can result from this disease. There is a vaccine for whooping cough, diphtheria, tetanus, measles, polio, cervical cancer, herpes, pneumonia, and others. All this is a result of medical research. Research must continue today and in the future to deal with the other illnesses that affect the quality of our life.

Arthritis is an area that is being researched vigorously to find ways to deal with this disabling and sometimes-crippling disease. New drugs have been discovered. Before, all that patients were able to take for the pain was aspirin; now there are many newer drugs to help the arthritic patient. Non steriodal anti inflammatory (nsaid's) are helpful, but newer drugs are on the market such as Celebrex, Bextra, Vioxx, and Mobic. Some of these are no longer used, but research continues on other drugs. I am sure that newer and better drugs will become available in the future. This will affect many people, especially the older population, and it is hoped that research will find new and better drugs.

Chapter Twenty-Two
Legal Problems

I started medical school in 1951, and during that time I have been exposed to the remarkable growth of knowledge in the medical field. The improvements in surgery, drugs, and treatments that have developed in just 54 years have been remarkable. Now I ask you, why is there so much criticism against doctors? Why are there so many frivolous lawsuits, and so much negative propaganda against doctors? Lawyers and patients are quick to file lawsuits and destroy many innocent physicians' reputation and finances. Some lawsuits are justified, but many are not. Having a lawsuit filed against a physician raises the cost of his malpractice insurance and damages his reputation even if he wins the suit.

In the meantime, what have lawyers done in this same time period to help humanity? All they have accomplished is to find new ways to sue, new things to sue for, the use of class-action suits, and developed new and innovative ways to increase their fees.

I'm talking about trial lawyers who prey on their victims. It has gotten out of hand! These costs do not come free; they are passed on to the consumer and the doctors. The cost of health insurance, and the cost to all patients for any type of medical care has increased. It probably runs in the billions. All this in spite of the fact that most cases that go before a jury are dismissed as unjustified by the jury. In addition, when an award is given, the lawyer often receives as much money as the patients. Why should lawyers share in a jury's award? They suffered no injury.

In 1960 when I started my practice, malpractice lawsuits were unheard of. The cost of malpractice insurance for me at that time was $500 dollars a year. When I retired, the cost had risen to $100,000 per year for surgeons. Today I've heard of some premiums, especially in the practice of obstetrics and gynecology as high as $250,000 per year in the state of Florida. Talk about inflation! The main reason for all of this was the sudden attraction to lawyers as a way to get rich quick.

I'm not saying that there is no malpractice, but I'm sure it happens a lot less than the lawsuits filed. Doctors can and do make mistakes, but today more care is given to avoid malpractice, and in general, physicians are better trained than they were in earlier years. If malpractice does occur, I believe that the patient has a right to fair compensation. I don't think that a lawyer is entitled to 35-40% or more of the award. What's wrong with a fair, hourly charge per hour for an attorney? They say that it costs money to try their cases; okay then, pay their costs and then charge a fair, hourly charge. Lawyers say that their time is money, and for that, they should be paid. What about doctors and all of the time that they put into charity work that they perform? Is their time not valuable? Legitimate cases deserve legitimate judgements but not so that the lawyer can charge outrageous fees.

A pet peeve of mine is frivolous lawsuits won by lawyers with charisma that are great actors in front of a jury. They don't necessarily deal with the truth; they just convince a jury that whatever happened to the patient or his family somehow or another is always the doctor's fault.

I'll give a couple of examples: a well known lawyer allegedly has made 40-60 million dollars in his career suing for the parents of babies born with cerebral palsy. This is a sad event in the mother and child's life, but is the birth of the defective child the fault of the doctor who delivered him or her? The answer in these cases is no! Their assumptions are based on erroneous information that they use to convince a compassionate jury that the doctor must be punished. They claim that if a cesarean section had been done that a normal child would have been delivered. After all, seeing one of these children makes the jury feel that there has been malpractice and that the doctor should be punished. The truth, based on good evidence, is that cesarean section does not prevent cerebral palsy. The juries give very large awards not based on scientific evidence but based on a lie. The lawyer can convince a jury that what he tells them is the truth and can show the defective child as their evidence of this gross injustice perpetrated on their client. They can then win the lawsuit. In the meantime, cesarean sections are not without more risk to the woman and her child. The c-section rate when I was in training was no more than 6%. Now the rate is more like 24%. Doctors are afraid to risk lawsuits for not doing a section, so they do more of them. There are more complications with the increase in sections. Where is the logic in that?

Another example of a legal scam was when the legal profession caused Dow Corning to file for bankruptcy because of the avalanche of lawsuits filed as a result of so-called complications from the use of implants that contained silicone. Many jobs were lost, and a legitimate company was destroyed, again based on erroneous information. It seems that many women who received breast implants produced by Dow Corning had multiple and varied complaints allegedly produced by the silicone used in their implants. Some of these complaints may have been legitimate, but most were not. Just the suggestion that silicone could be a problem produced symptoms in some less-than-stable women. Some that had saline implants even produced symptoms. Now years later, the research has shown that the implants are safe, and they are again being approved by the FDA for use in breast augmentation surgery. The problem is that the damage by greedy lawyers too anxious to make money without the facts, has already been done.

Class-action lawsuits are a method that attorneys have used to enrich themselves. These vultures advertise on TV around the country to recruit people to join in to their lawsuits for various reasons. The end result is that the largest beneficiaries of this type of lawsuit are always the lawyers. They often manage to destroy a company, cause job losses, and enrich themselves. The so-called victims or people they represent often profit very little. The federal government is finally attempting to stop this abuse of the legal system. This is a much-needed reform.

The latest victims of these unscrupulous attorneys are the drug companies. Their attack is directed toward complications allegedly caused by some of the anti-arthritic drugs. One study used as an example was a study on a Cox 2 inhibitor called Celebrex. This drug has been very helpful in relieving symptoms of arthritis in many patients. The study was performed on 2500 patients aged 70 and above to see if the drug had any effect on the incidence of heart attack or stroke. It turned out that in three years on the patients in that study, there were thirty cases of heart attack or stroke. This study is ridiculous. If you take any 2500 patients aged 70 or above, not taking Celebrex or any other medication, I will bet you that in that age group that you will have at least thirty cases of heart attack or stroke. What is ignored is that no drug is 100% safe. There are complications even with aspirin.

I had to do a gastrectomy on a patient that ingested only one aspirin to keep him from bleeding to death. The complications have to be considered when prescribing the drug by the physician, and the patient has to be advised of the risks. The decision is then made whether or not to prescribe the drug if the benefits out weigh the risks. The important factor that is overlooked is that many patients do experience relief from their pain and suffering while taking these drugs. The drugs Bextra and Vioxx have been taken off the market and are now being investigated. I wouldn't be a bit surprised to see them reappear on the market if the lawyers haven't already destroyed the drug companies. They have to spend untold millions to defend themselves. That money could be better spent on research to develop new and better drugs. Putting a drug company out of business is not the answer, recognizing the side effects of the drugs, and making people aware of the risks while they can enjoy the benefits makes more sense. The patient and his doctor, then, being aware of the risks, can make their own decisions as to whether to use the drug or not. I've seen many patients who would take almost anything just to relieve their continual pain.

The reason we now have the availability of new and better drugs is because the drug companies continue to spend money on research and development. Better to spend the money on research and development than spending it to defend themselves in court and enrich the attorneys.

Frivolous lawsuits that have no basis in fact cost the insurance companies, the doctors, and patients untold amounts of money. Somebody has to pay for all of this, and guess who pays? It all goes back to the consumer, or in these cases, it's the patient who ends up paying higher fees just to cover their additional insurance fees and medical costs. Physicians have to increase their fees just to keep up.

Another way that lawsuits hurt financially is when doctors, just to cover themselves, order every test available that is in any way related to the problem. Most of these studies are not even indicated, but doctors order them just to CYA. If you don't order something, some lawyer is sure to pick the doctor apart in court and ask why certain studies were not ordered. Whereas, in some cases when only a simple x-ray is indicated, now a doctor will order an MRI, a cost of thirty dollars compared to one thousand, five hundred dollars.

When I went through training, students and interns were instructed to use very specific studies or tests for each condition in treating patients. You don't even have to be a doctor to order everything in the book. Anybody can just order multiple tests on a patient without giving any thought as to what it will take to treat or diagnose each individual patient's illness. In fact, in training, any doctor not being specific about what tests were related to each accident or disease, would be criticized and his grades lowered for not using his brain to order the appropriate studies.

Today, doctors are afraid to not order excessive studies. The cost of this is out of sight, but if they don't order everything, some attorney in court will nail him to the wall. The most important difference in doctors and lawyers is that doctors search for the truth, and lawyers just want to win their case and will not let the truth get in the way of winning.

I have been the victim of a frivolous lawsuit, so I know firsthand the anxiety and stress of going through a lawsuit. It affects your whole life. You and your family have the thought always in your mind, spend endless hours talking about it, spend many sleepless nights, and still have to defend yourself, while trying to continue practicing medicine. The fact that you know that you are innocent even makes it worse.

In those days, before our community had a plastic surgeon, I performed many breast augmentations (breast enlargements) using implants. It was easy and gratifying surgery, and there was quite a demand for this type of surgery in our area. I had many patients on whom I had performed this surgery that were very happy with the end results. The cost for just the implants, the sterile package obtained from the hospital, the nurses hired to work in the operating room, and the drugs used in the procedure cost about $800.00. It was our policy to collect in advance. Usually we were also paid our fee before we did the surgery. In the event we did not collect our entire fee, we at least wanted to cover our costs. After all, this is not emergency surgery, and even if I performed the surgery for no fee, I at least wanted to cover my costs.

I had a patient who came to me to do the surgery, and all of the details were explained to her several times. It was explained that she had to at least put up the money for my basic costs. She then told me that her father, only too well known to me, would guarantee payment. I told her that I could not accept that. (I knew that her father would never pay me.) I told her that it was no emergency, and when she got the money together, I would do the surgery. The surgery was cancelled two days prior to the scheduled date, and I scheduled three operations at the hospital on that date.

She came in on that day, and lied to my nurse that her father had made arrangements with me. I was in surgery at the time, so my nurse, not knowing the true story, kept her in the office until I could be contacted and the situation explained. After my first case, I responded to a call from my office. When I was told what had happened I was taken aback, to say the least, because we all knew what decision had been made two days before in the office. There was no way that I could have cancelled my surgery at the hospital to take care of someone in my office that had lied about our agreement made earlier. Well that did it! She got an attorney and sued me. It couldn't be malpractice, because I never even saw her or spoke to her on that day. Two and a half miserable years later, we finally got the case to court. It took the jury five and a half hours to come to a verdict, because one of the jurors wanted to give her something. They settled for $3050.00 dollars. Her lawyer nearly dropped his teeth. He was from Pensacola. It cost him two and a half years of work, cost my insurers a great deal of money to defend the case, and cost me, because my malpractice insurance later went up. Technically, I lost the case, because she was awarded $3050.00. We considered appealing, but it would have cost my insurer at least another ten thousand dollars just to defend the case, and it just wasn't worth it. This later became one of the reasons that I decided to retire early. Performing surgery is stressful enough without having to deal with lawsuits, especially when they are without merit.

In Florida today, we are dealing with a malpractice crisis. The cost for malpractice insurance, and the litigious climate is driving good doctors out of the state and causing others to retire. Many states have gone to a $250,000.00 cap on pain and suffering, and it has worked well to diminish the number of lawsuits filed.

Florida legislature, succumbing to the wishes of the attorneys, has chosen not to do so. This will come back to haunt them. The quality of medical care in the state will diminish, as some of our better, more qualified doctors leave the state. Fees are much higher than they should be to pay the high insurance costs.

In south Florida, some physicians have elected to go "bare" and have no malpractice insurance. They transfer their assets into their wives' names, and if they are sued, this will minimize their losses. The lawyers then do not have the rich insurance companies to go after for their multimillion-dollar awards. This is not right either. If a patient is wronged, some compensation is usually in order, but people must realize that medicine, unlike mathematics, is not an exact science. Doctors do their best to provide quality care, but have no control over the life habits of the patients that they treat. Some are smokers, alcoholics, drug addicts, etc. Some do not follow instructions or take care of themselves. This is out of the doctors' control.

One thought proposed recently may have some merit, based on the fact that most doctors are very conscientious and do the best that they can for their patients. Things don't always work out as expected. When it's not deliberate, doctors should not be punished for a bad result unless they have been negligent or unresponsive to a patient's needs. Doctors cannot guarantee perfect results every time. On the other hand, patients who have received injuries or certain unusual bad results based on neglect or incompetence should be compensated. Why would it not work if a system like workmen's compensation were developed, where cases could be reviewed, not by a jury without any medical knowledge, but by qualified physicians to compensate valid claimants.

This would take the lawyers out of the picture, and greatly reduce the skyrocketing cost of medicine. The injured parties would probably be better compensated rather than having to split their awards with their attorneys. I'm sure that physicians would rather pay into a medical compensation fund instead of paying outrageous malpractice costs, just to satisfy a few greedy attorneys.

Chapter Twenty-Three
Health Care

In the early days of medicine, doctors saw patients for low fees, or no fee at all. Medicine was and still is a very noble profession. Money was not as important to a physician as giving the patient quality care, achieving good results, a feeling of helping the patient, and the satisfaction that goes along with it. We took the Hippocratic oath very seriously.

I can't help but see what a dramatic change has come about in doctors fees. This to me is a very sensitive issue, and it goes back to my early days when my parents had to take me to a local doctor to be treated for a relatively minor problem. The doctor was very reasonable, but we were dirt poor, and when I saw what my parents had to pay for the office visit it made an impression on me in my practice.

From then on, I had trouble with charging high fees for my services. My office help was always after me to raise my charges. When I went to Bayou la Batre I would make house calls for $4 to $6 dollars. I knew that these patients could afford no more. And I just didn't have the guts to charge any more. Remember, as a medical student patients were charity and were never charged. Also in internship and residency, no fees were charged, so it was not difficult to go into practice and do a lot of charity work. My intent when I became an MD was to make a decent living (which I did), but not be insensitive to the needs of my patients, either financial or physical. When I retired, my charge for office calls (after 25 years of practice) was only $15 dollars, and post-op patients were never charged. It was included in the price of the surgery. Doctors, nurses, and their families were never charged. This was what we called "professional courtesy."

An example of my fees during my practice years will follow later and be compared to fees being charged today. Now, there are some good reasons why fees needed to be increased, but it seems to me that some (not all) doctors have taken advantage of the situation.

Malpractice insurance is one reason fees had to be increased. This applies primarily to the high-risk practices of surgery, obstetrics and gynecology, ear nose and throat, neurosurgery, orthopedics, urology, and other surgical sub-specialties. However no doctor is without risk, and as mentioned earlier, malpractice is another issue causing fees to rise. These surgical specialties had to increase their fees to survive, but most of the other less-risky practices in medicine took advantage of the malpractice crisis and raised their fees as well. It seems to me that many of these doctors in less-risky practices could charge a lot less because their malpractice insurance costs are so much less.

The cost of going through medical school, internship, and residency, setting up a practice, and paying office personnel has gone up. The cost of setting up an office has skyrocketed, especially if any expensive specialty equipment or x-ray machines were needed. When considering the increase in the cost of a medical education and advanced training, there is some justification for an increase in fees, but personally I think that some doctors have gone too far.

Some patients that cannot afford health insurance, just cannot afford medical care. Older patients have Medicare; people with a decent income can afford health insurance, and lower-income people can often be eligible for Medicaid. There is a group of people in between that do not qualify for Medicare, or Medicaid and cannot afford private health insurance, but these people need help. It doesn't mean that the whole health-care system needs to be revised into a humongous government health-care system that becomes an unacceptable burden on the taxpayers.

One concept that could work in helping pay for the health care of patients would be to give a tax incentive to doctors treating indigent patients. For example, for patients without health insurance, Medicare, or Medicaid, who need medical or surgical care, the physician could submit a fee and have it within the usual and customary fees charged. Let's say the fee for a surgical procedure was $1000. Then the doctor would do the surgery free of charge, but receive a $1000 tax writeoff (not tax credit). This means as far as the government is concerned it costs the government (in a doctor's highest tax bracket) only $350.

A doctor in the 35% tax bracket gets a $1000 tax write off. That costs the government $350 less in taxes collected, but that is better than the government paying $1000 for some type of social program that the government would pay as in socialized medicine.

Rather than a complete overhaul of the system, sometimes a compromise is the best solution. It costs the taxpayer less, benefits the doctor with a tax writeoff, and he fulfils a duty to take care of needy patients plus has the satisfaction that goes with it. I think that most doctors would be happy to cooperate with some combination of a new system for health care for our country.

Some trial lawyers are really not my favorite people. Now I do have some very good friends who are lawyers, and think the world of them and respect them. There is a difference in the philosophy of most lawyers and doctors. Doctors are trained to find the truth as it applies to their patients, and treat them accordingly. If any new procedures, techniques or new knowledge is found, it is published in the medical journals and shared with all other doctors. There are no secret cures or procedures. We share all new information, and it is to the benefit of all patients. Some trial lawyers (and I know that this is a surprise to many people) do not necessarily pursue the truth. To them, all that is important is winning their case, and they will go to any extreme to win. They will lie or use any excuse to get their client off the hook, even when they know that their client is guilty. This is an entirely different position from that taken by physicians. I have difficulty accepting this line of thinking.

Naturally I am 100% pro physician (as if you couldn't guess), but reflecting back to when I first went into practice, I see an alarming change in the overall attitude of some practicing physicians. Fortunately this is not the case with most doctors. Back then, good patient care, concern for the patients and their families, availability to take care of their needs, and strong emotional support were very important in the practice of medicine. It still is to this day, but other factors have come in to change much of this. In some situations, physicians treat their practice as a business, and some of the compassion and personal touch has been lost. Money and advance payment is a major concern. There is less attention to the patient's needs, and the patient often leaves the office with the feeling that they have not had a chance to fully explain their symptoms to the doctor. What is frequently missing is the personal relationship which is so important for a patient to feel and be at ease with their personal physician. It is sad to see this happening, and a lot of the mutual love and respect that was present in a doctor-patient relationship is disappearing.

Much of this is understandable. The physicians have an impossible demand on their time, and probably see more patients than they can comfortably see. They also must see more patients to cover the increase in the overhead to run their practice, the rise in the cost of malpractice insurance, and the need to meet their expenses. I am totally astonished at the fees charged today and what they were in 1960. At that time, for me in a surgical practice, malpractice insurance was about $500 dollars per year, and when I retired from the practice of surgery it had risen to $99,264.00 I said, "Hell, just round it off and make it an even $100,000.00." I couldn't believe it. It's no wonder fees have gone up! All doctors now use these reasons to increase their fees, however, even in practices that are not high-risk specialties. Malpractice insurance in the field of surgery and obstetrics and gynecology are in the highest risk group, and their fees had to go up. I still think about the fees charged in 1960 and see what they are today, and it is frightening.

Up until just a few years prior to my retirement, my charges for an office visit was $10.00. My fee for reducing a colles fracture, including putting on a cast, and follow up for six weeks was only $50; now it's over $1000. I used to charge $350 for gall bladder surgery, and now it runs close to $2000. It's quite a difference.

I see initial office visit fees as high as $340.00. How can this be? That fee was charged to me, and the doctor was not even in a high-risk specialty. I paid this fee, and there was no professional discount. In the years that I was in practice, we treated physicians and their families at no charge. We were pleased that they had enough trust in us to let us treat them. Money was the least of our worries. I always felt that the care of the patient was most important, and that if you practiced good medicine that you would make a good living. I do not like the impression much of the public now has that doctors are "money hungry." Unfortunately, sometimes this is true, and it takes away the feeling people used to have from a doctor of compassion and trust.

Sometimes being a retired physician has its downfalls. For example, because you know a great deal about medicine and surgery, it puts you in the position of seeing some bad medicine being practiced. When I was in practice, I knew who the good doctors were and who the marginal docs were. This is an advantage that most people do not have. I've seen patients in pain that needed a physician to care for them (not necessarily in an emergency) that have to wait weeks or months to be seen by the appropriate doctor as they are shuffled back and forth between specialists. Their anxiety and pain remains, and they know who they would like to go to, but they would not be accepted as patients without the referral of their personal physician. It's not right to put off a seriously ill patient for weeks who may have a life-threatening illness. This is not in the best interest of the patient, and is not good medical practice. It certainly is not like the old days.

Chapter Twenty-Four
Ethics

Have you ever gone to see a physician and wondered if he or she really understood the problem you went to see him about? This is a situation that seems to be getting worse in this country. There are many different factors that enter the picture. One of the reasons may be that the patient does not explain adequately the problem at hand, and the physician doesn't really understand the patient's problem. Another factor may be that the doctor is so busy and preoccupied that he or she doesn't take the time to try to understand the patient's concerns. Another factor is simple communication. Often there is a language barrier between the doctor and the patient that can occur with foreign medical graduates. Also, doctors don't always communicate with patients in lay terms that they can understand rather than trying to explain a complicated medical condition only in complicated medical jargon.

I think a patient needs to be very careful in choosing a doctor. There should be subtle factors considered, such as appearance, dress, and feelings of friendliness, concern, and education. A well-trained medical doctor has on display all of his credentials. Has he or she gone to a class-A medical school? What kind of post-medical school training does he have? Was it in this country, or was it elsewhere? How much experience does he have? In surgery, in order to learn, one must have the actual experience of performing the surgery, not just observing. Not all doctors get to perform in their training, and a patient has the right to inquire about experience and training, asking, "How many procedures like mine have you done?"

There are many well-trained, capable, foreign medical graduates practicing in this country, but there are some that are not. A patient needs to be careful before allowing a surgeon to operate on him. A few doctors get in trouble and then have to call for help. This is true not only with some foreign medical graduates, but with some poorly trained U.S. doctors. Hospitals and their medical staff do a pretty good job reviewing credentials on doctors new to a community. They check on their credentials, experience, and training before allowing a new physician to perform any procedures that he is not qualified to perform. This works well in communities where there is a large enough medical staff to oversee new doctors. Unfortunately, in many (not all) smaller communities, inadequately trained, or incompetent doctors apply for privileges that are granted with no supervision. The community is so anxious to get a new doctor in town that they overlook the obvious, that is, are they qualified to perform these procedures? To make matters worse, in a number of small towns, there is a high percentage of older people who are easily taken advantage of. I have seen some doctors doing surgery that they have never been trained for, often with disastrous results. I can say this, because I have been in the position of having to pull the fat out of the fire and come to the aid of the patient. This is not good medical practice, and it always angers me when this happens, but it's the patient who suffers if you don't come in to help.

I practiced surgery in Fort Walton Beach for twenty-five years and during that time I had my share of responsibility. I served as chief of surgery for twenty-two years, chief of staff for two years, and served on the executive committee for twenty-four years. We had the responsibility of making sure that patients received good medical care and making sure that the doctors on the staff stayed in line. There were times when a physician had to be reprimanded for his actions. On the executive committee we dealt with inappropriate behavior, such as coming to see patients while under the influence of alcohol or drugs. In some cases, we had to terminate the privileges of some physicians and remove them from the hospital staff. Some were given the chance to correct their problems, and some were not, depending on the seriousness of the offense. As chief of surgery, I had to review the training of new doctors who wanted to do surgery at our hospital, and review the aptitude of those practicing surgery. If they couldn't perform, their operating privileges were taken away.

One such physician whose operating privileges I took away for cause, brought me before the executive committee for review. He felt that I had no right to take away his operating privileges. I told him that as long as I was chief of surgery, he would no longer be able to do surgery in our operating room. Because of past experiences and his endangering patient's lives, I could no longer allow it. He threatened to sue me, and I told him, "Get your best hold." He never did sue, and he lost his privileges. He is still upset and angry with me to this day. It was a thankless job, but somebody had to do it, and I was stuck with it. Without rules and regulations, it would be chaos.

Chapter Twenty-Five
Last Years of Practice

In my last year in practice, I gave a good deal of thought as to how long I would continue to practice. I was approaching twenty-five years in practice and lived through many changes over those years. I had gone from practicing in a 25-bed hospital with two operating rooms to a 250-bed hospital with eight operating rooms. It became more difficult to be able to schedule surgery because there were so many doctors using the operating rooms. Malpractice insurance had gone out of sight, from $500 dollars a year to $100,000.00 per year. Difficult and interesting cases you no longer scheduled because of the higher incidence of complications and the greater possibility of lawsuits. You do not have to be a bad doctor to be sued, just have a less than perfect result, and a litigious family, and you are open for a lawsuit. Add that to the higher cost of overhead to run your office (approximately $100,000 a year) and $100,000 a year of malpractice insurance, and it is no longer worth the risk a surgeon has to take.

There is also the risk of exposure to hepatitis, AIDS, tuberculosis, and other infectious diseases. To survive in practice, I would have had to greatly increase my fees, and I just didn't have the heart to do that. You get down right paranoid, and you feel like with any surgery that you do, you've got a lawyer looking over your shoulder playing a game of "gotcha." I loved doing surgery, but I was getting burned out with the litigious atmosphere in practice, and decided to call it quits. I never went into the practice of medicine to get rich. I sincerely felt that I wanted to help people, and if I practiced good medicine, I could make a comfortable living. That was enough for me, and it is far different from what it is today. I really enjoyed my career in medicine, and really enjoyed doing surgery, but I'm not sure if I had to do it all over, that I would choose to go into that field again. After my last year, and evaluation of my position, I sadly closed the door to that chapter and the practice of surgery.

There is life after surgery, though, and it took a big leap for me to find this out. For years I had some interest in real-estate development. This was a part-time hobby that I was able to follow, time permitting. It all started with an interest in apartment development that later proved to be profitable. It allowed me to retire from medicine and not starve. Initially I had a partner who was a contractor, and we bought a piece of land together and developed some apartment units.

Later he found himself in a financial bind, and he asked me to buy him out, which I did. Later I acquired a contractor's license and proceeded to build several more apartments with me as the general contractor. This was a hobby that was quite satisfying. Turning a bare piece of ground into a complex was very gratifying. It was an interest that was not only challenging, but was profitable as well.

In addition to acting as developer for the apartments, I later, after retiring, became interested in motel development, condo conversions, building an office building, and land development. I did this over a period of several years and enjoyed the challenge.

I did not enjoy the challenge of rebuilding motels after a storm. Our properties were destroyed by two tornados and four hurricanes in separate incidents. Fortunately, I had a very capable, hard-working, intelligent wife who worked shoulder to shoulder with me, and we struggled our way through some of these problems. We worked our way through these acts of nature that had inflicted severe damage to our properties. In spite of this, with a lot of dedication and perseverance, we survived successfully.

I mentioned earlier that flying was a big part of my life, so in addition to my flying days in the Navy, I got back into civilian flying in the early 1960s. A neighbor of mine, who was ex-military and was a flight instructor at the Destin Airport helped me decide. I had been out of flying for about ten years, and he convinced me to update my proficiency and start flying again. Because my time was limited, I felt that being able to fly would make it possible for me to travel and save a great deal of time. I flew all over the United States, Canada, the Bahamas, and even the British Virgin Islands. I finally gave it up at age 79. I had a Beechcraft Baron at the time, but I wasn't flying that much and just decided it was time to quit. I had accumulated 4000 hours of flying time, of which 1000 hours were actual instrument time.

At different times, I owned and flew 3 different Beech Barons, two pressurized Beechcraft Dukes, a Beech Bonanza, a Mooney, and a Merlin turboprop. I even checked out in a Lear jet just for kicks. I have many fond memories of my flying days.

Civilian flying is as a general rule very safe, but you must be prepared for emergencies in case all does not go well. One such incident happened to me one day as I was flying out of Gainesville, Florida. At that time, I was flying a Beechcraft Duke, which is a pressurized twin, and a very fine airplane. It could climb to 26,000 feet and cruise at speeds of 250 miles per hour.

After takeoff from Gainesville Municipal Airport, and as I was climbing through 4,000 ft., I heard a loud "bang" coming from the right engine. As soon as that happened, one half of my radios went out, the flaps trailed, the gear-caution lights came on, and the gear horn came on, indicating that the gear was not down and locked. At the same time, smoke started coming out of the right side of the instrument panel.

I immediately switched over to my good radios and called the tower, telling them that I had an emergency and was coming back to land. A cockpit fire in an airplane is one of the worst emergencies in flying.

As I let down, smoke continued to come out of the panel. It smelled like electrical wiring on fire. When I lowered the gear in preparation for landing, the green lights came on, signifying that the gear was down and locked. They came on momentarily, and then went out. At that time, I did not know if the gear was safely down or not, and I notified the tower that my gear on landing could collapse, resulting in a gear up landing.

They asked me if I wanted to fly by the tower and have them check it.

By then, the smoke in the cockpit was making it difficult to breathe and see out of the windshield, and I said, "Hell, no; I just need to get this airplane on the ground."

They said, "Take any runway; cleared to land."

On final approach, my wife had to be calmed down so that I could concentrate on landing the airplane. She was frantic, but I reassured her that the engines were still running and that we would get the airplane on the ground. I made the smoothest landing I ever made, and on the rollout, the smoke stopped coming out. They had the fire trucks and the emergency crew waiting at the end of the runway, and as I stopped, I told my wife to get out of the airplane. She did, and since the smoke had cleared, I told the tower that I was going to taxi the airplane off the runway to the parking ramp. I did this very carefully, knowing that the gear probably was not fully down and locked, and could collapse at any time. I found out later that the gear was down, but not locked in place. It went down with such force, that it had hit the stops and bounced back, making it totally unstable, and if I had not made a smooth landing, it would have collapsed.

After arriving at the ramp, I had to consider my options. I needed to get the airplane to Birmingham for repairs, and for a short time I considered flying it back myself, but then I thought that I better not do that. I called the Beechcraft factory for advice, and the airplane was one week out of warranty. In spite of this, they said that they would repair the problem at no cost to me. They were very honorable people to deal with. They sent a pilot and mechanic from Birmingham to fly the airplane back for repairs. They were going to fly back with the gear wired down and take no chances of the gear not functioning properly when they had to land.

At that time they really did not know what the problem was. They attempted a takeoff, and as the pilot applied full power, the whole right panel burst into flames. They immediately aborted the takeoff, taxied back in to the ramp, and reconsidered their options. On their second attempt, they were able to take off with the gear wired down, all belts to the alternator cut off, radios off, and using a handheld radio. This time they were successful in flying the crippled airplane back for repairs. They found that there was a defect in the alternator that caused a short. Systems that were designed to run on a 24-volt system were exposed to 120 volts, resulting in the wiring being burned. Beech Aircraft was good to their word, and paid for the $38,000 in damages. I was glad that I didn't attempt to fly it back myself. Out of over 700 Beech Duke airplanes produced, this was the only cockpit fire that was ever recorded in that type of airplane. Lucky me! All was well that ended well, and it was another of life's interesting experiences.

For recreation, we would spend a week or two in the mountains of Colorado snow skiing. It was fun to get together with several doctor friends and their wives. We skied at Steamboat Springs, Breckenridge, Vail, Keystone, Crested Butt, Winter Park, Lake Tahoe, and Aspen. We learned to ski quite well, even skiing most of the expert slopes, and getting on the slopes from the opening of the lifts in the morning until they closed in the late afternoon. All went well for many years, but nothing is forever. I used to watch over our group, and make sure everyone made it down the slopes, and help those who were not as proficient to find their way down to the bottom.

One day, it snowed all day, and I had on an old pair of skis, which were shorter, and I thought more maneuverable in all of that snow. While standing on top of one of the steep slopes, in that whiteout, I had vertigo, and my skis started to slide apart, and I started to slide down the hill. At that time I felt two of the ligaments in my left knee snap. The bindings never released. I tried to ski, but my ski stayed in place while my leg turned. I had to be taken down to the first aid station by the ski patrol, by a girl that couldn't have weighed more than 100 pounds. I asked her if she could handle taking me to the bottom in a basket. She said she could handle it, so I said, "If you lose me, head the stretcher to the nearest bar."

This was the year that the entire area had a severe snowstorm, closing all of the airports, and there I was with my left leg in a long splint, snow all over the highways, and my airplane over one hundred miles away. We managed to get back to Denver, after several detours because of the deep snow, only to find the airplane covered with snow. We had to wait two days before the airplane was cleaned and the airport runways cleared so that we could leave. Fortunately, one of my friends, Les O'Steen, who was with us on the trip was also a pilot, and he drove us back to Denver. He was then able to fly the airplane back to Destin.

After I got home, I contacted an orthopedic surgeon friend of mine, and arranged for the surgery to repair my injured knee. I had torn the medial collateral and anterior cruciate ligaments, one of which had to be repaired with a tendon graft.

Two weeks after my surgery, I had gotten restless, and my wife took me to the hospital operating room to visit my friends. While there, the only surgeons in the hospital were involved in a major surgical procedure and could not be available for any emergencies. A patient arrived in the emergency room with an acute appendix, and since I was there, they asked me if I could or would do the surgery. I agreed, and went into surgery standing on one leg with the other in a long, leg cast that I used for balance. All went well, and patient and doctor survived the procedure. After I finished, another emergency came in, and I was asked to do another case. I agreed; just a glutton for punishment, but as a physician, you do whatever you need to do.

After I retired from the practice of medicine in 1985, I stayed busy taking care of my properties, and continuing with development of a motel. I traveled 600 miles a week doing this. It wasn't nearly as stressful as doing surgery, and it kept me quite busy. My wife and I kept up our exercise by walking three-four miles five days a week. While practicing, there was little time for exercise, and I was pleased that I was able to expand my exercise program after that.

One day while walking up a hill, I began to experience chest discomfort (no pain). I stopped to rest, and my wife wanted to go back to the house, get the car, and take me back home. After a few minutes, I felt better, and didn't want her to go back to the house, so we finished our four-mile walk. A few days later, the same thing happened, so I rested and returned home. I couldn't believe it was my heart, so the next day I got on my treadmill, was only able to stay on for three minutes, and the discomfort reappeared.

I went to see my good friend, Dr. Russell, and he made arrangements for an angiogram in Pensacola. We did not have the facilities in our local hospital at the time. After the angiogram, I was immediately admitted to the hospital and was seen by a cardiac surgeon who was a friend of mine, and an excellent surgeon. I had 90-95% blockage in the anterior descending artery, which provided 70% of the blood flow to my heart. Complete blockage meant death. He was worried about me, and put me on the operating schedule as the first case the following morning.

He did a triple bypass, and all went well. After five days in the hospital, I went home a very lucky man. Fortunately I had no heart damage, because of the presence of numerous collaterals. I was able to resume all activities after my recovery. I was able to qualify to keep my pilot's license from the FAA one year after my surgery. The FAA required extensive studies and a stress test to maximum, which I easily passed. Since then, the FAA has required complete lab work and a stress test every year. The following ten years, I took a stress test every year, and all to maximum and all normal. I owe my life to my friend, the vascular surgeon. Now I know what it feels like to be on the other side of the knife.

Chapter Twenty-Six
Medical School Reunion

On May 19 to 22, 2005, I celebrated my 50th medical school reunion from Tulane University School of Medicine in New Orleans, Louisiana. I had been looking forward to this reunion for some time. At Tulane, traditionally there is a reunion for each class every five years. We were the class of 1955, with originally 134 students. There are 90 of us left, and the rest have all gone to the great hospital in the sky.

Our home is 265 miles from New Orleans, and my wife, Becky, and I drove to the Crescent City. It's not a bad four-and-a-half-hour drive. We went to our favorite (very old) hotel, the Fairmont, and checked in for our stay.

The hotel originally was built as the Grunwald Hotel in 1893, and after extensive remodeling in 1923 became the Roosevelt, in honor of Theodore Roosevelt until 1965 when it became the Fairmont. It is one of the oldest grand hotels in the country. Eight U.S. presidents have stayed there, among them Presidents Coolidge, Eisenhower, Kennedy, Ford, Bush, and Clinton. Others that have stayed are royalty and world leaders and Hollywood celebrities. A 60-million-dollar renovation restored the hotel's original grandeur, especially in the lobby, with a mixture of Italian, French, and African marble. It's a grand old hotel, and brings back memories of some time that I spent there while attending medical school. Some of the functions were held there, and I was also able to see stars like Sid Caesar, Jerry Vale, and others.

One of the highlights of the trip was a class dinner at the Windsor Court Hotel. Approximately fifty of our classmates out of the ninety remaining showed up and enjoyed the dinner. After dining, we were each individually asked to stand and tell our classmates what had happened and what we have done since graduation from medical school. We heard some very interesting stories.

Most of the class members had retired from the practice of medicine. They had practiced in various specialties of medicine throughout the Midwest and eastern United States. A few were still in the active practice of medicine and some still raising kids. Our oldest member was 83, and at age 79, I was the next oldest in the class. We had both spent time in the service before going to medical school, and most of the class was between the ages of 72-75 and had spent all of their life in the practice of medicine. A few went on to become well-known medical-school professors, and one became the dean of a well-known medical school.

The first two years of the medical school used to be located at the uptown Tulane Campus on St. Charles Avenue across from Audubon Park. The entire school has been moved downtown across the street from the Hugh 3000+ bed charity hospital.

My wife, Becky, and I went back to the original campus to see the old buildings, and just reminisce, and talk about old experiences on that beautiful campus.

On the last day of our meeting, our class met in the Blue Room at the Fairmont Hotel for breakfast. We were pleased to hear from two honored speakers. One was Ian L. Taylor MD, the Dean of the School of Medicine, and the other was Paul K. Welton, senior vice president for Health Services. Their presentations were very exciting and stimulating. We were told about research and experimentation that was going on at the school. They talked about gene therapy, stem-cell research, primate lab studies, new advances in cancer research, and other subjects. It is remarkable how far medicine has advanced in just fifty years.

After this, one of our classmates, Henry Pitot, received the lifetime achievement award that was well deserved. He is Professor Emeritus of oncology, pathology, and laboratory medicine at the McArdle Laboratory for Cancer Research at the University of Wisconsin. Dr. Pitot has published over 400 research papers, review articles, and book chapters. He has served in leadership positions on many national medical boards and has received many outstanding awards. He is also a nice guy, and I am happy to have been one of his classmates.

The next item on the agenda was the presentation of our second medical school diplomas, and a fiftieth reunion medal given to each of us by our two distinguished speakers. All in all it was a very pleasant experience being with my old classmates.

I feel very fortunate to have had the opportunity to practice in this area, as the first and only surgeon for many years. It has been a rewarding experience, and I'll never forget it. I've seen the hospital grow from 25 beds to almost 300 beds. I was the eleventh doctor to come to this community. Now there are over 400 doctors and medically related specialties in this area. This includes eleven general surgeons, fourteen plastic surgeons, orthopedic surgeons, ENT surgeons, urologists, neurosurgeons, Ob/Gyn doctors, ophthalmologists, and vascular surgeons. The number changes as new doctors arrive. The medical field has come a long way since the early days of medicine and surgery in this county.

Chapter Twenty-Seven
Final Thoughts

As one gets older, it's nice to look back and reflect on memories from the past. Some are good and happy, and some are not. It is not always easy to remember all of your patients after operating over a period of thirty years. During that time, a busy surgeon will have operated on thousands of people. You can't possibly remember all of them.

One story I like to tell is that while out socializing or meeting people out in public a the patient who comes to you and says happily and gratefully, "Do you remember me?"

Then I look up at someone six-foot-four, and honestly say, "No I do not."

He says to me, "You took my tonsils out when I was five years old."

All I can say at that time is, "You have really changed a lot since then, and I'm glad that you have done so well."

Most patients are appreciative and remind me of their experience with their surgery, and their good, long-term results. I knew a well-known, respected gentleman in our community who never failed to tell me that I helped him to stop smoking. He always thanked me for that effort. There are others who, after years of smoking and my trying to get them to quit, show up with a cancer of the lung and then tell me how much they wished that they had listened to my advice. Sometimes it is just too late.

I'm sure every doctor is approached by patients when they are out at a social event, who ask many questions related to their health. Often it is such an obsession that they will not let you socialize with others, and will monopolize all of your time while at the party. Usually you are polite, and answer their questions as best you can without a physical examination, and let it go at that.

I had one lady who, at every social event where we were both present, would latch onto me and go through the same routine. It's not that she couldn't afford a medical consultation at the office; she was very wealthy. Finally one day I had heard enough, and we were surrounded by people. So I told Mrs. X that if she would take her clothes off right now that I would be happy to examine her and give her a medical opinion then and there. That finally put a stop to her cornering me at every party.

Now that I have retired, at age 80 I am enjoying a well-deserved rest as payback for all the years of hard work, night calls, emergencies, and difficulties that I faced in the early days. I live comfortably in Destin, Florida, with my wife and my cat. I keep myself entertained with reading, some social life, and golf. Life has been full of interesting and satisfying experiences.

Author as an apprentice seaman with a scalplock haircut done for a $5.00 bet and by a roommate who was previously a barber.

Winter carnival at Dartmouth College, February 1944. Ice statue with dormitory in background.

Another statue at Dartmouth College. Symbol of Dartmouth is an Indian with a scalplock.

Training in SNJ (advanced trainer) climbing into the cockpit.

Banana River Naval Air Sation group that went through training in F6F's prior to being assigned as fighter pilots on aircraft carriers. Left to right, top: Bill Harris, Berle Brown, Instructor Whitey Holmguard, Ted Kennedy. Bottom row: Gene Celano, Jack Bernard, Burke Dunlap, and G.P. Kinney. We called ourselves "The Barflys."

Aircraft carrier #32 USS Leyte. Our home away from home.

Two F8F Bearcat flying in formation.

Carrier operations: F8F landing, notice the cable attached to the tail hook, stopping the airplane.

Carrier operation: F8F taking off.

Carrier operation F8F taxiing forward after landing.

Author flying F8F #214 over Quonset Point, Rhode Island, in the winter.

Fellow pilot on flight deck leaning into the wind during a hurricane in the North Atlantic in 1947.

Reminiscing at the Naval Museum in Pensacola, Florida looking at a beautiful F8F admired by me.

This was at the Naval Museum in Pensacola, Florida. Here are two types of airplanes that I had flown; the Corsair and F6F Hellcat.

This is a brand new ensign with his first new car.

First medical staff at Fort Walton Beach Hospital top row: Joe Wilson, Dr. Anderson, Jerry Hollingsworth, Author Gene Celano, Fred Crews. Bottom row, left to right: Bernard Russell, Bill Thompson, Drew Gieson, Henry White, Bob Maxon, and Fred Caldwell.

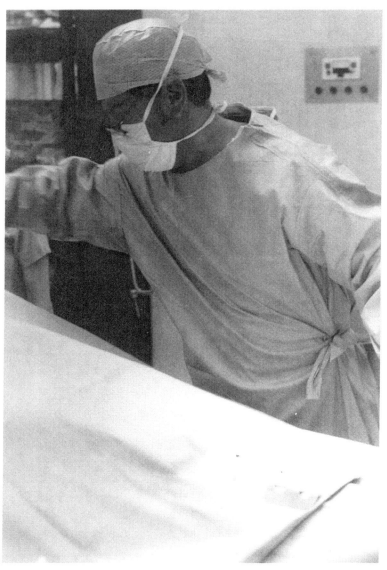

Author preparing for surgery.

This woman thought she was still pregnant after two years.

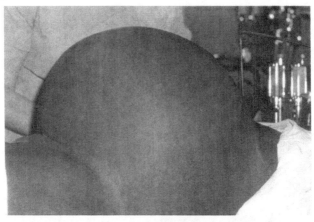

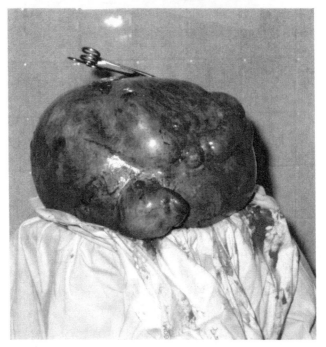

An 84 pound overian cyst removed from patient's abdomen. Pictures before surgery shown in picture above.

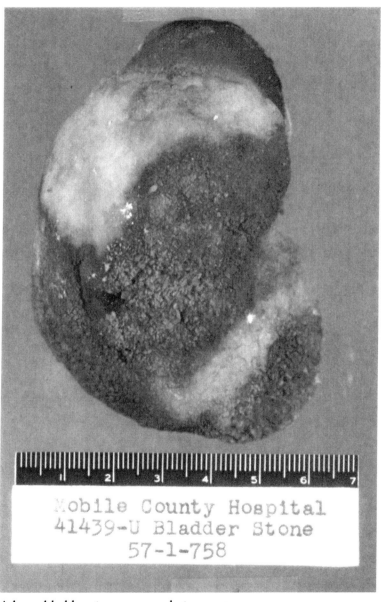

A huge bladder stone removed at surgery.

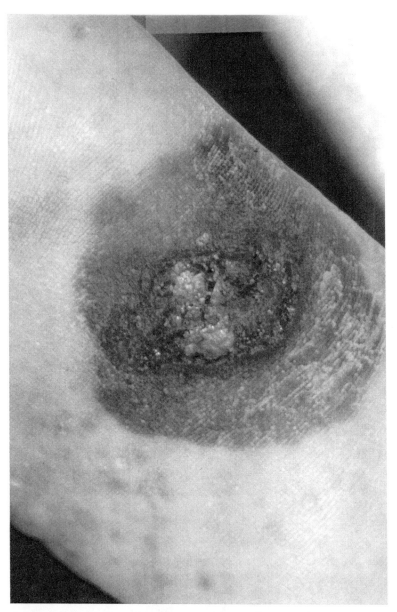

A large well-developed malignant melanoma.

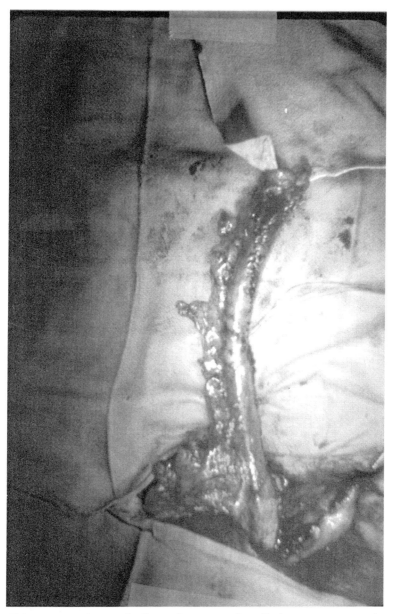

This was a tube made from the stomach called a reverse gastric tube to be used as a replacement for a severely damaged esophagus. One of three operations used for this purpose.

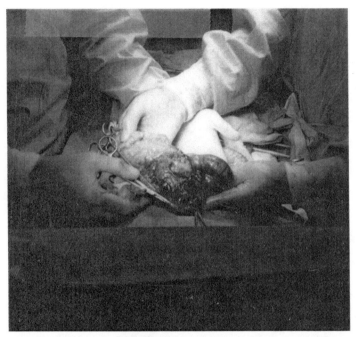

The removal of diseased bowel.

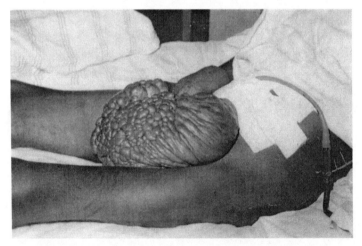

The end result of advanced gonorrhea, enlarged scrotum with multiple fistulous openings.

CPSIA information can be obtained
at www.ICGtesting.com
Printed in the USA
LVOW12s1333100217
523870LV00001BA/35/P